Old Faithful Inn

Crown Jewel *of* National Park Lodges

by Karen Wildung Reinhart
and Jeff Henry

Roche Jaune Pictures, Inc.
2004

Published by Karen Wildung Reinhart and Jeff Henry
Roche Jaune Pictures, Inc.
171 East River Road
Emigrant, Montana 59027
406.848.7912
rochejaune@imt.net
wildhart@imt.net

All text written by Karen Wildung Reinhart except
chapter nineteen written by Jeff Henry. Captions written
by Jeff Henry. All contemporary photographs by Jeff Henry
unless otherwise noted.

Back cover Haynes photograph courtesy Harry Child II.
Inside front and back cover Old Faithful Inn blueprints by
Robert C. Reamer, courtesy F. J. Haynes Blueprint/Map
Collection, Montana Historic Society, Helena, Montana.

The authors' research into the history of Old Faithful Inn is
ongoing. Any information or historic photographs would be
greatly appreciated. Correspondence regarding the Inn can
be sent to the above address.

Book design by Adrienne Pollard
Pollard Design/Black Mountain Press
Livingston, Montana
blackmtn@mcn.net

Printed and bound in China.
Printed on acid-free paper.

ISBN 0-9679814-2-5 (clothbound)
ISBN 0-9679814-1-7 (softcover)

We dedicate the book

to Harry Child and Robert Reamer,

the men who gave Old Faithful Inn

its auspicious beginning.

We extend an equal heartfelt dedication

to all Inn employees and guests

who share our love for

the log and shingle treasure,

Yellowstone's Old Faithful Inn.

ACKNOWLEDGEMENTS

A special thank you goes to Lee Whittlesey, Carol Shively and Roger Anderson. Their support, insights, and careful editing of this book were greatly appreciated. We are deeply indebted to them all.

The following libraries and archives (and their staffs) were of great assistance: Yellowstone National Park Research Library, Archives, and Photo Archives, Mammoth, Wyoming; Montana Historical Society Research Library, Archives, and Photo Archives, Helena, Montana; Montana State University Bozeman Library, especially Merrill G. Burlingame Special Collections; Park County Livingston Library, Livingston, Montana; Yellowstone Gateway Museum, Livingston, Montana; Park County Historical Archives, Cody, Wyoming; and the Newberry Library, Chicago, Illinois.

Many people made significant contributions to this book. We would like to thank the following individuals for their stories and their assistance: Bob and Peggy Adams, George Ainslie, Kristen Arsenault, Mike Ayler, Jim Baerg, Dave and Joyce Baltz, Richard Bartlett, Jim Bechtel, Andy Beck, Bob Berry, Roxanne Bierman, Jeane Blackburn, George Bornemann, Shawn Bready, Leon and Nancy Brunton, Blue Bunch, Bruce and Jacqueline Calhoun, Gary Carter, President Jimmy Carter, Beth Casey, Bob Cash, Diane Chalfant, Al Chambard, Lynn Chan, Bill and Loretta Chapman, Alissa Cherry, Betty, Sabra and Harry Child II, Lynn Christensen, Jim and Pat Cole, Maurice Colpitts, Allen and Jean Crawford, Tara Cross, Jon Dahlheim, Jack and Susan Davis, Cathy Dorn, Richard Dysart, Andy Edmisten, Mary Fenner, Margie Fey, R. Paul Firnhaber, President Gerald Ford, Gary Gebert, Susan Glenn, Robert Greer, Tom Griffith, Tom Hallin, Bonnie Hammer, Ken Hansen, Betty Hardy, Diane Harper, Bev and Cliff Hartman, Henry Heasler, Carlene Heller, Jack and Roberta Henry, Tamsen Hert, Jo Ann and John Hillard, Rick Hoeninghausen, Harold Housley, Myron Huntsman, Roberta Hurtt, Ginny Irvine, Katherine Jensen, Ann Johnson, Miriam Johnston, Phoebe Karnopp, Ken Keenan, Jeannie Keeter, Cynthia and Mike Keller, John Kennedy, Shari Kepner, Darren Kisor, Susan Kraft, John and DeNette Landrigan, Chris Larcinese, Duncan Large, Holly Lehmkuhl, Margaret Levy, Chuck Lewis, Steve Tustanowski-Marsh, Pierre Martineau, Robert and Virginia Mautino, James McDonald, Warren McGee, Gaylord Milbrandt, Tim Miller, Joe Mitchell, Charles Mullins, Mary Murphy, Dan Ng, Nancy Ost, Mike Parshall, Fred Paulson, Jim Peaco, Larry and Betty Perkins, Gwen Peterson, Adrienne Pollard, Eleanor and Patrick Povah, Leslie and Ruth Quinn, Brian Raines, Amy Recker, Donna and James Reed, Emma and Forrest Reinhart, Roy Renkin, Margie Replogle, Nick Ricardi, Glenn and Wanda Roberts, Joyce Roberts, Tom Robertson, Eric Robinson, Homer Rudolf, Steve Rumley, John Salvato, George Sanborn, Steve Sanders, Karen Selleck, Don Shaner, Bob, Duane, and Karen Shelhammer, Brian Shovers, Carlos Smith, Robert Smith, Eleanor and Tom Stone, Melissa Stringham, Rosemary Succc, David and Kathy Summerfield, Denny Sutherland, Joe and Lorraine Swift, Shannon Taylor, Steve Tedder, Hill Theos, Sally Thompson, Wayne Tilley, Marty Tobias, Judith Turck, Elizabeth VanderPutten, Mark Watson, Tammy Wert, Doris Whithorn, Tamela Whittlesey, Donelda and Glenn Wildung, Bill Young, Barb Zafft, and Evelyn Zimmerer. Please forgive us if we have accidentally omitted anyone.

(Photos previous two pages and above ©Jeff Henry)

Old Faithful Inn is an icon of both Yellowstone National Park and the entire national park system. It established the style of park lodge architecture that now typifies many scenic regions of the American West, and as such it continues to represent history and culture in Yellowstone. Architect Robert Reamer seems to have understood this when he designed the building to exhibit its own strong presence in order to strike a balance with the potent imagery of its setting, so that the new Inn could enter into a powerful union with the nearby geyser basin.

Of course Yellowstone National Park is itself iconic. It is the first national park in the world, cornerstone of conservation history, exalted example of wilderness preservation, linchpin of early tourist travel to the American West, and a member of the first family of mythical places.

The opening of Old Faithful Inn in 1904 unveiled a signal moment in the history of both architecture and national parks. "Perhaps for the first time in American architecture," wrote Merrill Ann Wilson about that event, "a building became an accessory to nature." According to historian David Naylor, the new building marked a passage in architecture from rough functionality to a consciously developed rusticity. Old Faithful Inn was the prototype for all such rustic buildings that were later to appear in national parks, a style that became famous as "parkitecture." The 1984 National Park Service "Draft Development Concept Plan" stated that the Inn's harmoniousness with the adjacent wilderness setting "served as a model for the National Park Service in succeeding decades."

From Mrs. Edward Johnson in 1905 ("We had such a jolly time!") to Cathy Baker Dorn in 1970 ("Oh, my God, my heart stopped!"), decades of Yellowstone visitors have been enthralled by Old Faithful Inn. These enthralled visitors are best exemplified any day of the summer season by heads and eyes turned upward and mouths open in the Inn's lobby. Indeed, Inn employees know that first time visitors can be easily identified, because they are the ones "looking up."

Now for the first time, two longtime Yellowstone residents, Karen Reinhart and Jeff Henry, have thoroughly researched and written a complete history of Old Faithful Inn. Their book reveals in great detail the answers to the obscure history questions and long-wondered-about mysteries of this famous building.

We have needed this book for so long in Yellowstone. During my thirty-plus years in the Grand Old Park, I have constantly heard questions about the Inn, questions for which none of us had answers. As one might imagine, surmises and assumptions were made about these questions, and incorrect notions abounded. While two tentative pamphlets on the Inn have long been available, the deep story has not been spaded until now.

Now Karen and Jeff have done the research and have put many of our questions to rest. For clues to the past, they located and cited obscure newspaper articles, rare journals and diaries, and little-known photographs. They interviewed many (sometimes-aged) former employees and examined their scrapbooks to mine the insights of those observers. They have added greatly to the wonderful start made by guides Ruth and Leslie Quinn who figured out locations of the original rooms in Old Faithful Inn and pursued information on architect Robert Reamer.

Join us now in enjoying the first deep history ever produced about Old Faithful Inn. I think I speak for Inn lovers everywhere when I rejoice in stating that it is so nice not to have to wonder any more.

LEE WHITTLESEY
Yellowstone National Park Historian
June 26, 2003

"All of beaut[y], all of great art...
the essence of both is gratitude."

—FRIEDRICH NIETZSCHE, GERMAN PHILOSOPHER, 1888

MILLIONS OF PEOPLE have walked into the lobby of historic Old Faithful Inn over the past one hundred years. Their heads tilt back as eyes look up and up and up—in an instant they become smitten with the creative grandeur of the lodge. Wonder and awe of how such a distinctive structure was built—within the wondrous setting of Yellowstone National Park—may creep into their minds.

Behind all human-made objects of beauty lie stories of creative inspiration, hard work and appreciation. With the driving force of the railroad and concessionaire entrepreneurs, the leadership of expert architect and crew, and the skilled employees that make it all possible, the

4411. Lobby, Old Faithfu

Inn has responded to the needs of the Yellowstone visitor. It has been expanded and adapted but has remained the framework for countless impressions, stories and adventures. Old Faithful Inn has charmed a multitude of lives and is remembered by nearly all who have walked through its massive red doors.

Since the opening of Old Faithful Inn in 1904, this hostelry of simple luxury has stood the test of time in a land of extremes: high altitude heat, cold, snow and wintry winds have religiously assaulted its towering presence. Further challenged by

owstone National Park

its location on the enchanted ground of the Upper Geyser Basin, the Inn has survived the effects of earthquakes, wildfire and the homage of millions of visitors. The Inn's foundation of lichen-covered volcanic boulders parallels the geologic groundwork that sets the stage for all of Yellowstone's stories: her thermal features and the myriad of wildlife and plant species that together make up Wonderland.

CHAPTER ONE

Yellowstone's Hallowed Earth

*"We see Nature working with enthusiasm like a man,
blowing her volcanic forges like a blacksmith blowing his smithy fires,
shoving glaciers over the landscapes like a carpenter shoving his planes,
clearing, ploughing, harrowing, irrigating—ever working toward beauty higher and higher."*

—JOHN MUIR, 1898[1]

OLD FAITHFUL INN has undergone an array of changes, varying in degree and suddenness. Today, the visitor beholds an Inn that has evolved as a result of these processes. Old Faithful Inn unfolded from its foundation skyward and so has Yellowstone National Park. The park's impressive geysers owe their water and steam display to the geology underfoot. Their "roots" go deep and tap unseen power. To fully comprehend the Inn's tale, we must begin from the ground up and give credence to the "place" of Old Faithful Inn. The sacred ground of Upper Geyser Basin is like a partner to the Inn. Together they draw millions of people to the boardwalk and threshold.

Yellowstone's story is an ongoing chronicle of geology. The park was carved by glaciers and sculpted by some of the world's largest volcanic

Scalding water from Old Faithful Geyser explodes into the frigid air of a bitterly cold winter morning. *(Photo ©Jeff Henry)*

eruptions. Yellowstone is perched above a "hotspot"—a plume of molten rock or magma that is perhaps only three to five miles beneath the surface. The last cataclysmic eruption occurred 640,000 years ago.

The approximately 10,000 thermal features of Yellowstone are proof that the volcano is not dead. Yellowstone National Park personalizes geology—visitors can actually see the earth's processes at work in nature's classroom. A visitor can observe hot spring pools, alive with colorful heat-loving bacteria, chuckle at the comical mud pots, and feel the awesome power of the geysers. Scientists believe that someday—perhaps thousands or hundreds of thousands of years from today—the Yellowstone volcano will erupt again.

Congregation of cow elk
in autumn near Castle
Geyser, with steam from
other thermals in the
Upper Geyser Basin
in background.
(Photo ©Jeff Henry)

As people stroll on the boardwalks of the Upper Geyser Basin, they regard nature's displays of earthly unrest as Old Faithful Inn's first visitors did, yet these thermal features are constantly in a state of flux. Minor earthquakes occur in Yellowstone daily and are the harbinger of change just beyond the Inn's doors *and* beneath its floors. Bellhop Shari Kepner lives on Bat's Alley, the fourth floor of the "Old House," (the original Inn, before the East and West Wings were built). The Inn truly is tied to the ground on which it stands:

> *When I'm lying in bed reading,*
> *sometimes I can feel the Inn shake.*
> *It moves and shakes a lot. It is not*
> *the carts rolling on the floors below,*
> *I do not think it is the wind, rather*
> *I think it is geyser activity. I haven't*
> *figured out which geyser it is yet.*[2]

Visitors to the park can observe earthquake activity on a seismograph at the Old Faithful Visitor Center. Geologist Robert B. Smith says "earthquakes keep Yellowstone alive,"—seismic activity flushes the mineral buildup from thermal features' plumbing systems. Earthquakes and their expressions of heat, water, and pressure are the reasons Old Faithful Inn is where she stands.[3]

The sacred ground of the Upper Geyser Basin is like a partner to the Inn. Together they draw millions of people to the boardwalk and threshold.

The most famous
geyser in the world
holds a nearly
mystical attraction
for Yellowstone's
visitors.
(Photo ©Jeff Henry)

Gary Carter's painting "Roche Jaune"—Rocky Mountain
trappers or mountain men were the first Euroamericans to see
the wonders of what is now Yellowstone National Park. The
mountain man pictured here in Gary Carter's famous painting is
riding along the rim of the Grand Canyon of the Yellowstone
River, his horses wading through the first snow of early autumn.
(Painting courtesy Gary Carter, West Yellowstone, Montana)

CHAPTER TWO

Entice, Explore, Protect

*"We encamped and set some traps for Beaver and staid 4 [days].
At this place there is also large numbers of hot Springs some of which have formed cones of
limestone 20 feet high of a snowy whiteness which make a splendid appearance
standing among the ever green pines."*

—OSBORNE RUSSELL, TRAPPER, JULY 11, 1838[1]

LONG BEFORE MOUNTAIN MEN CAME TO THE YELLOWSTONE REGION, Native American people had hunted game during the warm summer months. Archeologists believe indigenous peoples have lived in the Yellowstone region for about 12,000 years. Spear points and tools have been unearthed at ancient campsites along Yellowstone Lake; some were dated about 9400 years before present.[2]

Trappers and mountain men began to trickle west by the 1820s driven by a desire to find furs and freedom. Historians credit former Lewis and Clark Expedition member John Colter as the first European American to see some of Yellowstone's curiosities. Colter traveled on foot and was alone in a wild and wide country.[3]

Hundreds of ambitious, adventurous men followed in Colter's footsteps, mainly in pursuit of the beaver and its coveted pelt. Jim Bridger and other trappers related tales of the geothermal wonders of Yellowstone. Some stories were branded "outright lies" but continued to circulate and entice nonetheless.[4]

Scientific explorers, lured by wondrous tales, began traveling to Yellowstone in 1869. In the same year, the first railroad to span the breadth of this country was completed, linking the tame civilized ways of the East with the wilds of the West. Factual and fanciful accounts of this unusual land of geysers were written and advertised back East. These written words along with travelers' new-found mobility, served to entice scientists as well as the American public toward the sunset.[5]

Scientific explorers coined many of the park's place names even before Yellowstone National Park was established. After keen observation of various thermal features, their shapes, perform-ances and personalities, these men gave clever names to the park's unique manifestations of subterranean hot water. Old Faithful Geyser, so named for its impressive regularity, was one of many features named by the Washburn-Langford-Doane Expedition in 1870. Thirty-four years later, an Upper Geyser Basin hotel would take its name from perhaps the world's most famous geyser, the Old Faithful Geyser.[6]

Yellowstone's unique attributes had begun to be sung. Less than seventy years after Lewis and Clark's historic journey west, people and devel-opment began to settle the Rocky Mountain region. Without protection, resource use could begin to negatively impact the region's thermal features and wildlife.

The incredible power of Old Faithful Geyser (discharging between 3700 and 8400 gallons of water per eruption[7]) and other thermal areas of Yellowstone could have been developed for personal gain. Hydrothermal resources could have powered industry, sealing off a natural appreciation of geysers and colorful bacterial mats. Hot spring resorts could have dotted the high plateau of Yellowstone. But none of that happened.

Funded by Congress, the Hayden Geological Surveys explored the Yellowstone region four times beginning in 1871 and contributed rich scientific and artistic proof of Yellowstone's wonders. The Hayden Surveys were supported in part by the Northern Pacific Railroad; together they helped pave the way to preserva-tion of the world's first national park.[8]

Fortunately in 1872, Yellowstone National Park—the world's first—was set aside for future generations to protect and appreciate as Mother Nature might have intended. From the begin-ning, Yellowstone's legacy for people the world over was to help them embrace nature through preservation and appreciation of its wildness. This "balancing act" of resource protection and visitor enjoyment was at the very core of legislation that created the National Park Service in 1916.

Two of the very earliest western explorers made a tantalizing reference to the area that is now Yellowstone Park in 1806. Reviewing what they had learned about the Yellowstone River, Lewis and Clark wrote in their journals that "the indians [sic] inform us...there is also a consid-erable fall on this river within the mountains." This is one of the earliest historic notes referring to a feature in what is now the park, and there can be little doubt that Lewis and Clark's Indian informants were alluding to the Upper and Lower falls in the Grand Canyon of the Yellowstone River. The Lower Falls are pictured here.
(Photo ©Jeff Henry)

Bison cow and calf feeding by Castle Geyser in autumn. Located a short distance down valley from Old Faithful Inn, Castle Geyser was quite likely one of the large geyser cones described by mountain man Osborne Russell in the quotation used to open this chapter.
(Photo ©Jeff Henry)

Hot spring resorts
could have dotted
the high plateau
of Yellowstone.

Wonderland Becomes a Pleasuring Ground

"It is a region of wonder, terror and delight. Nature puts forth all her powers, and her moods are ever changing...Here tremendous geysers shoot up their mighty fountains...hot springs, indescribable in their strange beauty,...pools of seething mud, casting up jets of colored paste, bewilder by their curious activity. The Park unfolds a succession of pictures, each more striking than the other."

"How may the wonders of the Yellowstone National Park be reached? Practically there is but one route. The Northern Pacific Railroad remains, and probably will remain, the only direct...route to the Park."

—QUOTES FROM NORTHERN PACIFIC RAILROAD BROCHURE, 1885[1]

A. BART HENDERSON, a rough but literate gold prospector, first penned the term "Wonderland" in his journal as a reference to Yellowstone's unusual landscape in 1871; this name predates "Yellowstone National Park" as nomenclature. Later Northern Pacific Railroad advertisements helped cement "Wonderland" as Yellowstone's nickname in the minds of travelers.[2]

Railroads promoted the west's resources as they inched across the United States. With the creation of Yellowstone National Park in 1872, railroads promoted the park as well. The American public perceived dangers in the untamed west; the hardships of travel in Indian country were not to be taken lightly. Railroads nurtured the spirit of western adventure by easing the journey's adversities. Wonderland visitation began to climb; one thousand people journeyed to the park annually between 1877 and 1882.

Generations of tourists have found the promised land of Yellowstone Park just inside the Roosevelt Arch in Gardiner, Montana. President Theodore Roosevelt dedicated the arch that bears his name in April of 1903, the same year construction commenced on Old Faithful Inn. Photo ©Jeff Henry)

Beginning in 1883, wealthy visitors could travel on the Northern Pacific Railroad's park branch line up scenic Paradise Valley. Yearly visitor counts immediately quintupled. People wanted to experience the curiosities of Yellowstone first-hand, and travel by rail was a dependable and expedient way to get there. Railroads brought people west and once there, adequate transportation, accommodations and services were needed to serve them. Railroads were the driving force behind the creation of these travel necessities.[3]

Until 1916, most tourists to Yellowstone traveled by railroad to one of the park's gateway communities, where they boarded stagecoaches for the trip into the park. This coach was photographed in the Mammoth area, and probably was carrying visitors who had ridden the Northern Pacific Railroad to its terminus in Gardiner. The jubilation displayed by the passengers also indicates that they had just entered the park.
(Photo courtesy Thomas J. Hallin)

The standard-gauge park branch began in Livingston, Montana and concluded at the Cinnabar terminal, three miles northwest of Gardiner and the park's north entrance. Paralleling the Yellowstone River, the railroad spur was framed by the Absaroka Mountains to the east and the Gallatin Mountains to the west. The railroad laid the final stretch of track to Gardiner, Montana in June of 1903.[4]

Visitors marveled at wildlife and mountain scenery from a special passenger train aptly labeled the *Yellowstone Comet* in the 1920s. The train ambled along at 25 miles per hour and featured two open-air "rubberneck" cars. Simple wooden chairs faced outward and enticed the train's customers with unfolding western vistas and abundant wildlife. Regularly scheduled passenger trains delivered summer park visitors through 1948. The last special passenger train left Livingston for Gardiner in 1955.[5]

Beginning in 1901, the Burlington Northern offered transportation to Cody, Wyoming and beginning in 1908, the Union Pacific carried visitors to West Yellowstone, Montana. Like the Northern Pacific, both of these railroad companies offered Yellowstone tour packages.[6]

Tourists who rode to the Northern Pacific Railroad terminus were taken by 20-34 passenger six-horse drawn and wrangler driven "tally-ho" stagecoaches to the Mammoth Hotel. There they purchased coupons to sightsee by either two-horse surreys and wagons or four-horse coaches[7] for five and a half days for around $50, including lodging and meals. These "couponers" bedded down at three or four hotels during their travels within the world's first national park. Just five miles from the railroad platform, the Mammoth Hotel was their first night's destination. A hotel in the Lower Geyser Basin was home for the second and third nights. The Lake Hotel was their resting place on night four (beginning in 1891) and a hotel near the Grand Canyon of the Yellowstone was the place of repose on day five. Finally, visitors traveled back to Mammoth for their final night in Wonderland, bringing them full circle.[8]

Visitors frequently complained about their rigid predetermined touring schedule. The renowned Upper Geyser Basin was offered only on a half-day basis—not nearly enough time to casually stroll through the colorful geyser basin, peer into the seemingly endless blue pools, and feel the famous power of Old Faithful Geyser.

Visitors *could* stay at the Upper Geyser Basin to further explore the

The renowned Upper Geyser Basin was offered only on a half-day basis—not nearly enough time to casually stroll through the colorful geyser basin.

area at the magical times of sundown and sunrise, if persistent, *and* the other ten passengers were of like decision. However, the stagecoach driver would quote the additional expense required and warn them of the dubious comfort available. The first accommodations near Old Faithful Geyser were offered in 1883 and were simple canvas tents. Two years later, the "Shack" Hotel was built. This wood structure had muslin-covered stud walls which burned ten years later and was replaced by yet another ramshackle building. These early Upper Geyser Basin sleeping options gave visitors scant privacy, heat, and convenience.[9]

The closest hotel to the Old Faithful area, the Lower Geyser Basin's Fountain Hotel, opened its doors in 1891. It could accommodate 350 guests and was a vast improvement over its rugged two-story predecessor whose walls were flimsy canvas. Guests could enjoy steam heat and electric lights and revel in luxurious hot spring baths. The Fountain Hotel also featured a social life—gala balls where men could swing unattached ladies. But even the gregarious activities of the Fountain Hotel did not satisfy visitors who wanted to stay near the Upper Geyser Basin.[10]

Why wasn't there an adequate hotel in the Upper Geyser Basin? Because it was more than a day's ride for stagecoaches to reach the Old Faithful area from Mammoth. According to an early park tour schedule, stagecoaches lumbered along the primitive roadways between four and seven miles per hour but also took extra time for "stopovers" at interesting points. The Lower Geyser Basin accommodations were strategically placed a day's stagecoach ride from Mammoth. Other Yellowstone hotels had the same placement strategy of a day's drive between them, with lunch stations situated at halfway points of interest. Today's visitors tour the park by automobile in a fraction of the time it took early day visitors by stagecoach. Road junctions are evenly spaced throughout the park and serve as reminders of early day logistics.[11]

Early park regulations disallowed building any structure within one-quarter mile of a natural object of interest. Rickety Old Faithful Inn predecessors had blatantly ignored this rule. But when the rule was changed to one-eighth of a mile in 1894, this made it more appealing for investors to build a *legitimate* hotel near the

Upper Geyser Basin. Three years later, the Yellowstone Park Association's Superintendent of Buildings and Machinery, Mr. Bihler, drew up plans for an $81,000 hotel. The company planned to "move a portion of the Fountain Hotel steam plant and building...and much of its equipment...to the Upper Geyser Basin." Apparently dissatisfied with his design, the company hired architect A.W. Spalding to draw up new plans for a hotel one year later. The Department of the Interior approved his Queen Anne style hotel, but Northern Pacific Railroad directors disapproved it.[12]

In 1899, the acting park superintendent recommended that Yellowstone's system of hotels should include one in the Upper Geyser Basin. One year later, the assistant Secretary of the Interior voiced a like opinion. Park officials, as well as visitors, were exerting pressure for decent accommodations there. Increased stagecoach travel from the west also justified a decent hotel within a day's drive from West Entrance hotels.[13]

Sawmill Geyser erupting shortly before sunset. Sawmill was only one of the many geothermal attractions in the Upper Geyser Basin that created a demand for overnight lodging in the vicinity and ultimately led to the construction of Old Faithful Inn. *(Photo ©Jeff Henry)*

Absaroka Mountains, Montana
Northern Pacific Railway

Gustav Krollmann

Yellowstone "Comet" in Paradise Valley under Emigrant Peak. 1938

MONTANA

CHAPTER FOUR

The Northern Pacific Railroad and Harry W. Child

"Our air out in mountainous Montana and Wyoming...contains so much more oxygen, so much more verve, and is so much more invigorating that you can accomplish hard tasks and keep on accomplishing them."

—HARRY W. CHILD, C.1923[1]

Poster of Northern Pacific Railroad branch line leading up Paradise Valley from Livingston to Gardiner, Montana. The Northern Pacific financed the construction of Old Faithful Inn and other park hotels and publicized Yellowstone as a way of developing its passenger business.

RIGHT ABOUT THE VERVE, HARRY WAS DECIDEDLY WRONG ABOUT THE OXYGEN. The Northern Pacific Railroad had long been involved in the development of Yellowstone National Park's transportation and hotel industries, though in the past it had been a reluctant participant in the less profitable hotel business. The railroad sold its interests in the Yellowstone Park Association in 1901 in part to avoid building a hotel in the Upper Geyser Basin. The transfer of stock went to three men: Harry W. Child, and his two brothers-in-law, Edward W. Bach, and Silas S. Huntley—men the railroad hoped would sympathize with their interests.

One year later, Huntley's stock reverted to the railroad's holding upon his death and Bach sold out to the railroad, so only Child retained stock. Alone, Child lacked funds to build the long awaited hotel, but as president of the Yellowstone Park Association (and the Yellowstone Park Transportation Company), he thought it prudent to build a hotel near Old Faithful Geyser before his competitors could capitalize on a similar venture. He managed to obtain financial backing from the Northern Pacific Railroad and the reluctant railroad found itself back in the thick of things.

Harry Child was a highly successful businessman in Yellowstone and in the Bozeman and Helena, Montana areas where he raised cattle and owned real estate. Child was well connected with the railroad, and with Washington, D.C. politicians. He seemingly dreamed of monopolizing Yellowstone's concessions and eventually controlled transportation, hotels, lodges and tent camps. He would have run the park's stores too, but because the government wasn't keen on the idea, Child helped employee Charles Hamilton begin the Hamilton Stores dynasty (1915-2002). Together, Child and Hamilton also profited from gasoline sales in the park.[2]

Child was the key player in Yellowstone's glorious concessionaire era and his hotels were the apple of his eye.

8138. Rustic Depot at Gardiner, Entrance to Yellowstone National Park.

In an interview, former Superintendent Edmund G. Rogers described Child as "utterly ruthless," but in contrast author B. C. Forbes wrote, "Child was famous as a host, as a curer of the blues, flabby muscles, thin blood and other woes."[3]

The *Livingston Enterprise* ran several stories about Child following his death in 1931. One bold headline read: "Harry W. Child Dies in California Home—Death Comes As Climax to Long and Useful Life Devoted Always to Best Interests [in] Northwest Area." Child was the key player in Yellowstone's glorious concessionaire era and his hotels were the apple of his eye.[4]

Old postcard showing Northern Pacific Railroad depot just outside Roosevelt Arch in Gardiner, Montana. Excitement must have been high as tourists detrained, then boarded stagecoaches (tour buses in later days) for the long awaited entrance through the arch and into Yellowstone.

This 1910 railroad brochure shows tourists entering Yellowstone at the park's north entrance at bottom of card. The Upper Geyser Basin with the Firehole River, Old Faithful Geyser and Old Faithful Inn—the ultimate destination for many visitors—are illustrated at the top. *(Courtesy National Park Service, Yellowstone National Park Archives)*

Harry Child, early day Montana
businessman and hotel baron in
Yellowstone, was a prime force behind
the construction of Old Faithful Inn.
Photo probably taken about the time
Old Faithful Inn was constructed.
(Photo courtesy Harry Child II)

A youthful 29 in 1903, self-taught
architect Robert Reamer was
commissioned by Harry Child of the
Yellowstone Park Association to design
and build the Old Faithful Inn.
(Photo courtesy Richard Bartlett)

The Child and Reamer Team

"What's worth doing is worth doing well."

—HARRY W. CHILD, C.1923[1]

HARRY CHILD NEEDED TO FIND SOMEONE TO HELP MAKE HIS DREAMS COME TRUE IN YELLOWSTONE. To that end, Child discovered the talents of Robert Chambers Reamer in California, who was employed at an architectural firm in San Diego. A self-made architect from Oberlin, Ohio with only a sixth grade education, Reamer was 29 years old when Child brought him to Yellowstone National Park to design the railroad station in Gardiner and an inn at the Upper Geyser Basin. Reamer's use of volcanic stone and native timber in the railroad station foreshadowed his later projects in Yellowstone and Montana, beginning a fruitful career as "Yellowstone's Architect."[2]

With the rail wending its way toward the park's north entrance, Child envisioned a lavish train depot to serve his wealthy customers, to ease their transfer from rail car to stagecoach. A two-stagecoach-wide arch planned by the Army Corp of Engineers would beautify the park's north entrance and further entice visitors.[3]

While Reamer's career with park buildings would span thirty-three years, he didn't permanently live in Yellowstone, but spent time working on both coasts and in the Midwest. Reamer returned often at the request of

After twenty-one years of Upper Geyser Basin hotels of questionable quality, a distinctive and commodious hotel would finally be made possible by... railroad money.

Very early postcard of east side of Old House, photo taken shortly after opening of the Inn in 1904.

Another early view of the Inn, a colorized composition shot from the north, showing the red roof of the building's early days, with the original eight flags flying proudly above the widow's walk.

Child for both private and public commissions in Yellowstone and Montana. He is known to have designed over twenty-five structures. Most of them served as lasting legacies of his eclectic creativity and architectural genius.[4]

Reamer's daughter described her father this way: "my father lived for the pure joy of creating. He was forever searching for new ideas and when one appeared, it was cause for elation." Historian Richard Bartlett interviewed a local rancher who said, "workmen [on his buildings] compared Reamer with Charley Russell, the great cowboy artist and sculptor, who knew in his mind, precisely, everything he wanted in his painting down to the most minute detail." Reamer was also known to be modest and to have a good sense of humor.[5]

During 1903 and 1904—while Reamer pondered plans and directed the building of Old Faithful Inn—worldwide events were unfolding. Plans for the Panama Canal were in the news. Japan attacked Russian warships in Korea. Baseball's first World Series was played in Boston. Madam Curie became the first woman to win the Nobel Peace Prize. The Ford Co. sold its first automobile while Orville and Wilbur Wright flew the first heavier-than-air plane and after thirty years of digging, men completed the Hudson River tunnel to open railroad service between Jersey City and New York.[6]

A February 1904 newspaper article intoned, "A new hotel, Old Faithful Inn having accommodations for 250 tourists, will be completed at Upper Geyser Basin prior to June 1, this year. This will be the most artistic and comfortable hotel in the west, and is of rustic design."[7] After twenty-one years of Upper Geyser Basin hotels of questionable quality, a distinctive and commodious hotel would finally be made possible by—like the Hudson River tunnel— railroad money.

Wife of Harry, Adelaide Child was largely responsible for furnishing the Inn prior to its opening in 1904. *(Photo courtesy Harry Child II)*

The legendary construction crew of Old Faithful Inn posing on snow banks in front of the building in the spring of 1904,
presumably shortly before the Inn's opening on June 1 of that year. One of the profound mysteries in the history of
Yellowstone is how so little is known about the construction of the Inn, as well as how so little is known about the hardy
craftsmen who assembled this wooden work of art. One recently uncovered story, passed through the generations of
Harry Child's descendants and related by Harry Child II, has it that some workers on the Inn poached elk and bison in
the park. Skins and presumably heads of the animals were then hidden in the remote reaches of the uncompleted Inn
until they could be smuggled north to Montana, where they were sold to augment the workers' construction wages.
(Photo courtesy National Park Service, Yellowstone National Park Photo Archives)

The Construction of Old Faithful Inn

"It was my ambition to construct a building without a piece of planed wood in it. In all the big structure there is not a foot of smooth finished board or molding."

—ROBERT C. REAMER, 1905[1]

BEFORE CONSTRUCTION COULD BEGIN, timber needed to be harvested and supplies accumulated. The harvest of local building materials for construction of a new hotel was granted by the Department of the Interior in 1901. Child communicated to Northern Pacific officials in early December 1902 of his intention to haul lumber by horse-drawn sledge over snow to the Upper Geyser Basin—an experiment he hoped would prove far-sighted; heavily loaded wagons could mire in spring muck until late June, stalling progress on the new hotel.[2]

Reamer labeled his architectural drawings "Old Faithful Tavern," though even during the building phase locals branded the hotel "Old Faithful Inn." Reamer's blueprints were approved by the Department of the Interior on May 28, 1903.[3]

Perhaps the mystery keeps the *magic* of the Inn alive and well.

Even before Reamer's blueprints were given the "green light," Child borrowed money for the project. Yellowstone Park Association records have indicated that Child secured a $25,000 loan on March 18, 1903 from the Northern Pacific Railroad for Old Faithful Inn and for improvements on Lake Hotel. Less than two months later, he borrowed $50,000 more. These loans propelled his hotel projects forward—probably allowing the purchase of preliminary supplies—but by October 6, 1903, Child procured another $50,000 loan from the railroad. The railroad would eventually loan Child a total of $200,000 for both projects.[4]

Two clues have suggested where the new hotel's timber was cut. The only timber harvest noted by the Army stationed in the Upper Geyser Basin was on June 8, 1903: "patrolled south of station where timber is being cut for new hotel[,] distance about 8 miles." Lodgepole pine for the Inn was also harvested from forests next to the Mesa Pit Road above the Firehole Cascades north of Old Faithful. The Inn's construction reportedly began shortly thereafter on June 12.[5]

Perhaps the project had developed enough momentum to begin local timber harvest *before* June 8. Reamer wrote to a client a few years later: "Any logs that you wish to have the bark on, cut before the sap begins to rise." To satisfy Reamer's first floor requirements for unpeeled logs, perhaps workers did just that. Winter log-gathering over snowy frozen ground would have fit Child's scheme of "making hay while the skies snowed" *and* the logs would have undoubtedly suffered less from scrapes. Once the tree's life force had risen— about mid-May—greater care would have been necessary to protect the softer sap-filled logs from scarring. Men most likely hand-carried the logs to the waiting wagons during June harvest rather than skidding them with horses.[6]

The foundation of Old Faithful Inn, pictured here under the West Wing of the Old House. Reputedly quarried from cliffs above nearby Black Sand Basin, the masterfully crafted stone-work has supported the storied building for over 100 years. *(Photo ©Jeff Henry)*

Yellowstone's ubiquitous lodgepole pines, the primary building material used in constructing the Old Faithful Inn. Best records indicate that most of the lodgepole used in the building was cut about eight miles south of Old Faithful, but there is another indication that some logs came from the Mesa Pit area about 14 miles to the north. *(Photo ©Jeff Henry)*

Reamer used huge volcanic rocks to lend basal support to Old Faithful Inn, quarried from rhyolite cliffs near Black Sand Basin. After the Army located suitable rock for the new hotel, they inspected its procurement: "mounted patrol to Black Sand Basin to where masons are cutting rock." An igneous rock, rhyolite is a relic of the latest cataclysmic volcanic event in Yellowstone country. Just as Yellowstone National Park's awe-inspiring thermal oddities are its reason for existence, the historic inn too, is anchored by native volcanic boulders, giving it a profound sense of place.[7]

Several years later in another proposal, Reamer revealed his foundation strategy, evidently used for the Inn: "foundation will undoubtedly look better of stone if it is handled in an artistic manner...by carefully selecting the boulders for intended [place]. This should be laid with joints as far back from the face of the stone, giving the impression of a dry wall."[8]

After the foundation was laid, the massive rock fireplace and kitchen were likely fashioned next, probably in summer 1903, to provide workers with fireplaces for cooking, warmth and a blacksmith's forge. Perhaps the kitchen stove served carpenters warm nails to keep frostbite at bay, a clever strategy documented seven winters later during the building of the Canyon Hotel. Even so, frostbitten digits were thawed and doctored

This picture was actually taken in the winter of 1910-11, when freighters were hauling supplies to a hotel then being constructed at Canyon. This particular photo is used here because unfortunately no known photos of freighters hauling to Old Faithful Inn exist. But scenes identical to this one must have occurred during the winter of 1903-04, when similar efforts were made to supply the construction crews working on Old Faithful Inn. The challenges faced by these teamsters must have been almost unimaginable in today's world, as evidenced by the huge snowdrift blocking the road a short distance ahead of the horses. This scene was photographed at the Golden Gate, by Rustic Falls on Glen Creek, a few miles south of Mammoth on the way to Old Faithful. Robert Reamer, designer of Old Faithful Inn, is the man standing at left. *(Photo courtesy National Park Service, Yellowstone National Park Photo Archives)*

on site by a nurse during the Canyon Hotel project, evidence of the men's trials with disagreeable weather. The conveniences of electricity, steam heat and flush toilets were probably available to Inn workers by mid to late winter.[9]

Reamer used native rock and trees to properly seat Old Faithful Inn within its Yellowstone environment, but other building materials were imported to the job site. Plumbing, electrical and heating system parts and supplies, cedar and redwood shingles, nails and spikes, window glass, furniture, and more traveled from both the East and West coasts before final incorporation into the Inn. Supplies and food for workers and horses were also hauled many miles.[10]

Some of these materials and supplies were needed during winter. Arduous over-snow travel required horse teams, drivers, and heavy freight-bearing sleighs to deliver goods from the railroad station in Gardiner, Montana to the Upper Geyser Basin. Each journey with supply-loaded freighter and team took six days round trip. Seven years later, fifty drivers and two hundred

horses were required to transport *one* railroad car's goods to the Canyon Hotel building site.[11]

Small pine trees were used to delineate snow-packed roadways. The placement of these early "snow stakes" in broad, windy expanses like Swan Lake Flats south of Mammoth, was of critical importance: a misplaced hoof could send horses, wagon and goods floundering in the floury snow. Freighters' supplies to be hauled later were heaped in piles along the road like pioneers' abandoned goods from covered wagons heading west.[12]

Old Faithful Inn was further along that winter than some historians have previously thought. A photo of the Inn's construction—one of only two —clearly shows the Inn's progress as quite advanced in 1903. The framed-up walls and roof tower above the main floor's log construction. There is a revealing lack of snow indicating late summer or early fall. The bulk of the structural work was apparently completed before grueling winter weather set in.[13]

Though much of the remaining work was indoors, workers still had to contend with winter's inconveniences. Interior finish work including electrical, plumbing, and fancy wood and ironwork would have kept Reamer's team and contractors busy during winter. In early January, plumber E. C. Culley left Livingston, Montana for the Upper Geyser Basin to complete his contract on the new hotel.[14]

A winter visitor indicated the Inn's progress was advanced less than a month later:

The new hotel at the Upper Geyser basin is a marvel of beauty and comfort...Guests will be as comfortably located there as in the finest of the modern hotels in New York...The building will be completed in about thirty days...The kitchen is commodious and furnished with every modern contrivance known to the culinary art.

He also described in detail the Inn's lobby and dining room.[15]

An old stereoscopic slide, this is the only known photograph of Old Faithful Inn under construction. Indications in the photograph, including the fact that the ground is snowfree and dry, suggest that it was taken in the autumn of 1903. Indeed, there is a notation on the border of the slide that reads "Old Faithful Tavern 1903." This and other evidence points to construction on the Inn being fairly well advanced by the onset of winter in 1903, and perhaps belies the old notion that primary construction of the building occurred during Yellowstone's notoriously fierce winter. It is more probable that the Inn's hardy creators busied themselves with interior finish work during the winter, working inside the building's intact shell. *(Photo courtesy Bob Berry, Cody, Wyoming)*

The new Upper Geyser Basin hotel was never insulated, probably because it was never intended to be open during the winter. Even though the building was "roughed-in," it would have been a cold workplace in winter's "deep sleep." Frigid mornings and biting wind chills assaulted the titanic building—a mammoth amount of cordwood must have been offered the "fireplace gods." Winter on Yellowstone's volcanic plateau is not kind; ten feet of snow can accumulate and drift, burying familiar landmarks. Nighttime temperatures can plummet to hazardous lows. Brutal windchills can further assault human endeavors. Upper Basin Station weather records of the winter 1903-04 document 20 degrees below zero Fahrenheit, though it is uncertain whether these records are minimum temperatures. Between 1904 and 1960, the Old Faithful area averaged about 17 inches in snow depth and 17 degrees Fahrenheit in December. The record low during those winters was a sobering 50 degrees below zero Fahrenheit.[16]

Under the creative genius of architect Reamer, approximately forty-five hardy artisans of log, stone and iron erected perhaps this country's most famous western lodge. According to some authorities, some of the workers may have been "on loan" from the railroad, who had a vested interest in its timely completion.[17]

A circle of seasons passed while architect, builders and contractors worked their magic on the Inn. Why urge architect, journeymen, carpenters, blacksmiths and stone masons to wield their tools: pencil, axe, adz, hammer, saw, anvil and drawknife in the cold of winter? Time was of the essence for businessman Child and his railroad backers. Their goal was for Old Faithful Inn to welcome paying customers that rode the rails to Yellowstone by June of 1904. Perhaps local workers were eager to have otherwise scarce winter work.[18]

One thing is certain. These men were exceptional in their craft and their tolerance of difficult working conditions. A 1973 National Register of Historic Places Nomination Form noted:

> *Men of their stamp, possessing mastery of ax, adz and drawknife, independent and accustomed by their lifestyle to free use of their own initiative, can still be found today—but almost certainly not in sufficient numbers to so quickly build a structure of such dimensions and complexity...despite snow and cold.[19]*

Old Faithful Inn is certainly one of our nation's most important architectural icons, yet scant clues have been unearthed thus far about its craftsmen. (Blacksmith George W. Colpitts is the exception, see following chapter.) Bernard O. "Pete" Hallin, originally from Spokane, Washington, worked as a carpenter on Old Faithful Inn during its

construction. Ten years later, he supervised the construction of the Inn's East Wing for the Yellowstone Park Company. Thomas J. and Thomas Clyde Huntsman, father and son carpenters from Missouri, also labored on the Inn.[20]

More workers' names were discovered in an unusual way. Apparently, on April 23, 1904, a note was tucked inside the ball of one of the Inn's flagpoles. Fifty years later, it was found. Four workmen's names (H. Butler, C. Hasleman, W. High, and F. Carmody) were scribbled in pencil on a small piece of paper along with: "remarks—snowed like hell. Drank 4 quarts of booze. Can see about 118 poles." Though Inn builders accomplished a great deal in a short time, they apparently did take time off.[21]

One thing is certain. These men were exceptional in their craft and their tolerance of difficult working conditions.

Snow and icicles on the roof of Old Faithful Inn. This picture was shot in 1982 on the roof of the Pony Express Snack Shop. The large icicles are descending off the roof over the Inn's employee dining room and the scene includes Jim Peaco, now Yellowstone's official photographer, in an effort to give the composition a sense of scale. The scene is illustrative of wintry conditions at Old Faithful, and perhaps gives some idea of challenges faced by the 1903-04 construction crew. *(Photo ©Jeff Henry)*

Some of the workers also made time for clandestine activities. Betty Jane Child recalled a dinner conversation with Bernard "Pete" Hallin in the 1950s. She remembered Pete telling the following story:

> *The [builders] working on the Inn in the winter of 1904 would supplement their income by killing elk and buffalo —which was not allowed—and hide the hides in the far reaches of the Inn until they could get out to Mammoth and sell [them]. This was a good source of additional income to many of the workers.[22]*

Clues in other places have revealed who some of these men were. Engraved into the concrete patio under an Old House window are the initials "MLG" and the date "Oct. 6, 1903," a lasting testimony to one builder of the Inn. "Melvin Campbell" carved his name on a wall in 1903. A scrapbook margin identifies a "McManis" as a stone mason for the Inn's fireplace. During the fall of 2000, a workman's signature was found on one of the Inn's uppermost window frames. It was written in thick pencil—perhaps a carpenter's pencil— with the name "Albert Rock or Roch[e]" and the date May 7, 1904.[23]

Hopefully more accounts of these skilled men will emerge from the "woodwork" giving historians and fans of Old Faithful Inn a better sense of its story. Perhaps the mystery keeps the *magic* of the Inn alive and well. Old Faithful Inn captures the imagination of the park visitor like no other building in Yellowstone National Park and perhaps the entire park system.

But it wasn't only men who journeyed into the Yellowstone winter, experiencing its beauty and its difficulties. Adelaide Dean Child spent time in the Upper Geyser Basin with her husband Harry during the Inn's construction. The local newspaper noted: "H.W. Child, accompanied by his wife, is snowed in at the Upper Geyser Basin, it being impossible to get team [of draft horses] farther than the Golden Gate."[24]

And at least one other woman is known to have

Window pulled from extreme top of wall in Old Faithful Inn lobby in 2000. This window was removed for maintenance by Darren Kisor of a special crew that maintains historic buildings in Yellowstone. Darren spotted the signature and date seen here between the hands of Mark Watson, long time Yellowstone Park employee. Written in pencil, the inscription reads "Albert Rock (Roche?) May 7, 1904," and is a mysterious clue to the identity of one of the Inn's original craftsmen. Who was Albert? Where did he come from? Where did he go after the Inn was completed? These are questions that likely will never be answered. *(Photo ©Jeff Henry)*

been there during construction. According to late photographer J.E. Haynes, "Mrs. Robert C. Reamer lived throughout the winter of 1903-04 in Haynes Log Cabin Studio Building." The studio at that time was located in front of Old Faithful Inn. The *Livingston Enterprise* reported on May 7, 1904 that: "Robert C. Reamer was down from the Park today to take in the ball game and to meet Mrs. Reamer, who arrived Monday morning from the east." This is interesting, because the architect is known to have married Louise Chase on October 4, 1911. This evidence suggests that Reamer was married twice.[25]

Builders of the Inn used hand tools but also employed modern power tools of the day, such as power saws and lifts. The signatures of one-hundred-year-old tools have marked the passage of time—still visible on the Inn's walls. A steam-powered generator probably provided electricity for these tools and later supplied heat and hot water for Inn guests. These early generators were no doubt fueled by indigenous lodgepole pine.[26]

Reamer also utilized the predominant tree species of Yellowstone, the lodgepole pine *(pinus contortus)*. Throughout the Inn, lodgepole pine logs were used for beams, rafters, railings, posts, balconies, balustrades, staircases and decorative supports. The ceiling was veneered with pine slab wood— perhaps the leftover slivers from the Inn's flat sawn wall logs. A *Haynes Guide* noted "there are over ten thousand logs in its lower story."[27]

Old Faithful Inn has been called the "world's largest log structure." Indeed, the whole massive structure *appears* as though it is constructed entirely of log, lending support to the above claim. However, to dispel that myth, only the first floor of the Old House is constructed of load-bearing unhewn logs. The first floor is eleven logs high; each log was scribe-fitted and saddle-notched, requiring practiced and patient workmanship. Workmen tucked "oakum," an oily hemp rope between the logs to serve as chink, chasing away drafts and creating privacy.[28]

The second and third floors are constructed of a traditional wood frame—a construction scheme much lighter in weight than log. Both floors are cantilevered two feet beyond the first floor's perimeter, a design that would have been impossible with the continued use of log walls. The two upper floor's exterior walls are sheathed in half-log and cedar shingles respectively, in keeping with Reamer's vision. The shingles are 6" wide by 36" long. The lower two courses are laid out in a diagonally-carved chevron pattern, decorating the windows' top edge and the second level's bottom edge with a "fringe" of craftsmanship. This attention to detail is echoed handsomely within.[29]

With the exception of the north wall's large plate glass windows, Old Faithful Inn's windows and their panes vary whimsically in size and shape. Pane shapes creatively bounce among diamonds, squares and rectangles and emphasize Reamer's supposed desire to harmonize with nature's lack of geometric symmetry. For about twenty years, Inn tour guides have theorized that the assorted window sizes and shapes admit light into the lobby like "light through a forest canopy."[30]

The Inn also deviates from the human tendency toward visual balance—dormer placement on the great sloping roof is of an unbalanced nature. Historians and architects don't know the "why" of the tale but know the Inn was built to differ-

ent specifications from Reamer's original blueprint. His original drawing illustrates four small dormers flanking the row of windows to the east and two on the west. Their final placement is quite different from his blueprint, perhaps due to lighting and/or stair and landing requirements within.[31]

Of greatest curiosity are the two dormers on the sloping roof just above the third floor. They give the impression of functionality, but do not admit light into the lobby and were apparently built over the finished roof as mere decoration. The remaining windows and dormers above the third floor do not open up into guest rooms either, but they do send soft shafts of sunlight to the cavernous space below. Like any creative process, Old Faithful Inn evolved as its building progressed and Reamer's genius logically unfolded with it.

Early hand-colored Haynes postcards boasted a decidedly red roof. The roof's shingles were originally coated with a red mineral paint, believed to hinder flammability—a practice that continued through 1932.[32]

Closeup of detail on one the Inn's windows, with decorative chevron patterns cut into siding shingles. Patterns in window vanes show a great deal of variety throughout the Inn. *(Photo ©Jeff Henry)*

Early Haynes postcard
showing lobby and
fireplace in Old Faithful
Inn, illustrating the com-
plexity of interior detail
fashioned by architect
Robert Reamer's
craftsmen.

An important finishing
touch, this early Haynes
postcard shows the
Inn's original dining
room ready for its guests.
The plaited chairs were
crafted by the Old
Hickory Chair Company
of Indiana and are still
in use today.

CHAPTER SEVEN

The Inn's Finishing Touches

"three [train] carloads of furniture has [sic] already arrived for the hotels of Upper Geyser Basin and Lake— looking for one more [train] carload which is now on the road. They mean to have the hotels furnished in first-class up-to-date style, and everything for the convenience of their patrons."

—GARDINER WONDERLAND, MARCH 5, 1904[1]

THE AMOUNT OF FINISH WORK AND ARTFUL DETAIL given to the Inn by its creator and craftsmen is astounding. The assorted window pane shapes, clever building trim, porch and gable supports of gnarled lodgepole pine, and hand-cut shingles are impressive. These artisans of the early twentieth century apparently took their work seriously. Yet, there is also whimsy in the Inn's exterior and interior decoration. It's fun to behold the quaint ornamentation visible in every nook, on every floor, and in every room.

Reamer sketched instructions on a shingle and gave directions to his crew to find particular and peculiarly shaped pairs of pine branches. Subsequently, they searched for crooked limbs of lodgepole pine wherever they could find them. Reamer and his team of workers creatively matched up sets of similar bends and twists to create the lobby's picturesque pseudo-supports, giving the lobby its woodsy atmosphere. These contorted branches may have grown in response to insect and disease invasion (possibly caused by wounds inflicted by neighboring trees or wandering wildlife), or perhaps, by heavy snowfall.[2]

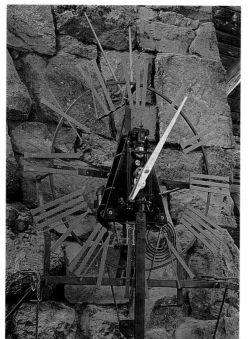

The compelling clock that has kept time for a century's worth of Inn guests and employees. *(Photo ©Jeff Henry)*

Reamer awarded the contract for the Inn's fancy wrought ironwork to George Wellington Colpitts in December 1903. Born in New Brunswick, Canada in 1855, Colpitts became a U.S. citizen in 1880, moved to Billings, Montana and learned the blacksmith trade there. He was eventually hired as a blacksmith in 1886 by the U.S. Army stationed at Yellowstone Park Headquarters at Mammoth, Wyoming.[3]

Colpitts hammered out the Inn's ironwork in his Livingston shop. But the Old Faithful Inn iron project was huge, prompting him to open a second shop in Livingston. He hired two additional men and also used space in a Gardiner blacksmith shop. A local newspaper reported: "Geo. W. Colpitts is hard at work on a dial, hands and pendulum for a large clock which will be placed on the outside [?] of the hotel in the Upper Geyser basin in the Park. The clock dial will be nearly five feet in diameter and the pendulum will weigh several pounds." Colpitts owned a traveling forge and probably did some of his ironwork on location.[4]

In addition to the great clock's ironwork, Colpitts also fashioned four sets of fireplace andirons, screens, tongs and pokers, and the popcorn popper. He hammered out the front door and dining room hardware, chandelier, porch ceiling lamps, electric candlestick lights that encircled log posts and illuminated guestrooms,

guest door numbers, hinges, knobs and mortise locks as well as the hefty wrought iron band that wraps the clerk's counter. According to his obituary, "[Colpitts's] fame as a craftsman spread not only over the United States but into Europe as well." This is true, no doubt, because Old Faithful Inn became loved as an icon of western architecture the world over—its ironwork trim a perfect complement to the building's preponderance of wood. Colpitts's iron art is a legacy that lives on today, pleasing the public as it did in yesteryears.[5]

Blacksmiths, sawyers and carpenters did much of the work on location—a practical and cost effective solution for the isolated project. Amazingly, Old Faithful Inn was constructed for only about $140,000—an absurdly low sum in today's world, especially considering the pleasure and comfort that it afforded so many visitors and guests since its beginning.[6]

Popular in America at the time, the Arts and Crafts movement influenced the choice of floor coverings and Mission Style furniture for the unpretentious Old Faithful Inn—comfort without excessive ornamentation. Child's wife Adelaide reportedly oversaw the procurement of furniture, rugs and curtains. The Yellowstone Park Company spent $25,000 to furnish the Inn's lobby, balconies, porch and original 140 rooms.[7]

George Wellington Colpitts with grandchildren. Colpitts was the blacksmith, based in Livingston, Montana, who wrought the Inn's fancy ironwork, such as the huge clock on the rock chimney and the rugged hardware on the Inn's front door. *(Photo courtesy George Bornemann)*

Another early postcard view of the west side of the lobby, showing the ornamented stair rail leading downstairs as well as the Inn's famous rock bubbler, near the entrance to today's Pony Express Snack Shop.

An early day postcard view of furniture on the Old Faithful Inn's second floor veranda.

Old Faithful Inn's furnishings had already been bounced by rail to Gardiner from lands afar. A newspaper article of mid-May revealed: "The hotel at Mammoth Hot Springs is filled with furniture, to be placed in the new hotel at Upper Geyser Basin." Ten days later, the newspaper reported: "Supplies for the various hotels have been freighted...through bad roads, snow drifts and under the most difficult of conditions.

The furniture for the Old Faithful Inn...is not yet completely installed."[8]

The Inn's lobby and balconies were outfitted with cushioned davenports, settees, armchairs, and rockers, probably made from oak and/or hickory. Substantial leather-topped wooden tables complemented the seating arrangements. Early photos show wicker chairs, rockers, and round wooden tables on the porch and veranda with spittoons conveniently placed for visiting gentlemen. Guest rooms boasted iron bedstead, wood-framed mirror, wooden table, chest of drawers, woven chairs and wash stand.[9]

Some of the original Mission Style pieces from 1904 still grace Old Faithful Inn. A few heavy oak wooden-armed davenports and chairs in the lobby are original to the Inn. Native to the upper floor bedrooms, the green octagonal tables now serve guests beverages on the second floor mezzanine. Today, a few original drop-front chests of drawers furnish Old House rooms. Refinished versions are used in the gift shop for display. Some of the original wash stands manufactured by Charles Limbert of Grand Rapids, Michigan still adorn rooms in the Old House for today's guests. The Old Hickory Chair Company of Indiana crafted the original plaited dining room chairs and those are still used today. Chair seats and backs have been rewoven as needed.[10]

Early postcards show double writing desks on the second floor balcony that have a more simplistic design than today's desks. Some of the attractive oak-partner writing desks in service today were listed in a 1929 furniture inventory. Each desk sports a green stained glass lampshade with copper overlay in the shape of pine trees and owl coupled with a privacy screen above. In the old days, visitors wrote letters and "souvenir postals" here, much as they do today.[11]

Over time, Old Faithful Inn's caretakers have acquired new furniture or have reupholstered and refinished furniture as needed. For example, in 1921, the Inn was the recipient of furniture that had once graced the Lake Hotel lobby. After the Inn's 1928 lobby expansion, the Lake Hotel furniture was reupholstered and four dozen new chairs were purchased as well.[12]

The rugs that softened the sounds and steps of guests were originally of the scatter and runner variety. They could be rolled up with ease to make way for dancing. Today, carpets and pads are tacked down to the maple floor that replaced the original pine floor in 1940. This second lobby floor is slated for replacement in 2004.[13]

The Inn's original rugs were probably woven cloth and possibly painted reed matting. One early postcard clearly shows a geometric diamond-patterned rug inset with leaves on the mezzanine floor. According to a 1929 inventory, floor coverings varied in fiber: grass, hemp, felt, wool, rag, cocoa, leathersteel and horse-hair. Keeping with tradition, the handsome rugs that adorn the Inn today are good examples of the Arts and Crafts style of the early 20th century.[14]

Other accoutrements rounded out the Inn's decorative statement. A "bubbler" or drinking fountain was crafted from volcanic stone to match the registration desk's foundation—both originally located in the lobby's southwest corner. Electric candlestick fixtures and chandeliers conveyed a pioneer sense in keeping with the rest of the building. The lobby's mail box was a miniature log cabin; the shoeshine stand was of rustic pine as well. On a "grand" scale, a piano promised to fill the Inn with music, as it does today during dinner.[15]

Old Faithful Inn is a log and shingle treasure.

The finishing touches were time consuming. An Upper Geyser Basin camper scribed in a diary on June 23, 1904: "went in big hotel...and is not finished." Just as architect Reamer expected that the Canyon Hotel would keep him "very busy until about July 1st," two weeks after its projected inauguration in mid-June 1911, there was undoubtedly last minute finish work to do following the Inn's opening date of June 1, 1904. Electrician M. Sullivan traveled to the park in mid-May 1904 to "be engaged for several weeks in wiring...Old Faithful Inn." Plumber E. C. Culley did not return from the park "where he had been installing plumbing for the new hotels" until late July 1904.[16]

Total cost of the construction and furnishings of Old Faithful Inn in 1904 was a paltry $165,000. That sum one hundred years later, would inflate to approximately 3.2 million dollars; even today, Old Faithful Inn is an incredible bargain. To compare, the nearby Old Faithful Snow Lodge cost $28 million in 1998. Though smartly constructed, Old Faithful Inn is far more compelling in its architectural statement than the newer hostelry. Today's architects intuitively knew the Snow Lodge should not and could *never* overshadow Reamer's vision—Old Faithful Inn is a log and shingle treasure.[17]

(Photo ©Jeff Henry)

8589. OLD FAITHFUL AND OLD FAITHFUL INN, YELLOWSTONE PARK.

COPYRIGHT. 1905. BY DETROIT PUBLISHING CO.

1905 postcard from west side of Old House.
Shot when Old Faithful Inn was only one year old,
park visitors can be seen in the distance near the
vent of erupting Old Faithful Geyser.

CHAPTER EIGHT

The Presence of Old Faithful Inn

"Suddenly...sitting in a pool of light was the most beautiful object I had ever seen in my life—
the Inn. Oh my God, my heart stopped. Upon entering the Inn I can remember going
round and round as I looked up and up and up...I swear it was the biggest
and most beautiful building I had ever seen."

—CATHY BAKER DORN, 1970, OLD FAITHFUL INN EMPLOYEE[1]

OLD FAITHFUL INN'S AWE-INSPIRING SIZE is perhaps the first thing a visitor perceives, even from the distant observation benches that circumvent Old Faithful Geyser. Seven stories high, the Inn's predominant feature is its steeply pitched, gabled and cedar shingled roof that reaches seemingly from the heavens down to the top of the second floor. Reminiscent of a plains skin tepee, the expansive roof communicates to visitors a profound sense of shelter. Perhaps the 10,000-foot peaks just beyond Yellowstone's high volcanic plateau inspired Reamer to match their majesty with this massive hostelry.[2]

We as human beings have a need to tame wilderness, but paradoxically we also need to retreat to wild places. Somehow, by surrounding ourselves with nature's bounty and beauty, we are restored. Old Faithful Inn acts as a bridge between the two worlds of wilderness and civilization, offering comfort in the midst of the rugged unpredictable world of geysers, hot springs and wild beasts. An early day visitor wrote of the veranda's view: "You see before you, both 'Hell' and 'Heaven,' [and] for once you can have your choice."[3]

Elk, bison, coyotes and other animals roam at will throughout the Upper Geyser Basin, attracted by the year-round foods available because of its ongoing warmth. While at Old Faithful and from a safe distance, visitors can experience wildlife from boardwalks or from the comfort of the Inn itself. Like a sentinel guarding the valley below, the grand old hotel stands watch over Mother Nature's wild, weird and wonderful.

If the roof's cedar shingles were like icing on a cake, the eight flags that unfurled at the Inn's apex in 1904 from its 12½' x 70' railed platform —were the candles. Early day guests could access this observation deck by hiking up through the lobby's expanse. During the Inn's opening year, traveler Clifford Allen noted:

> *Some of the party climbed to the lookout on top of the hotel and viewed the situation from that point with the aid of… field and opera glasses. This was no mean climb in these high altitudes.*[4]

This lofty lookout has been called by some the "widow's walk" named after early New England coastal homes equipped with widow's walks, though early Inn visitors scanned for geysers and bears instead of husbands returning from whaling adventures. A teenage resident fantasized one moonlit evening in 1913:

> *I dreamed I was on a tall ship playing a faraway sea. 'There She Blows!'…my reverie ended and it was only Old Faithful I was staring at, filling the night air with steam.*[5]

In the Inn's early history, flags and decorative pennants flew over it. In addition to the United States flag and the state flags of Idaho, Montana, and Wyoming, two read "Upper Geyser Basin" and the last two appropriately "Old Faithful Inn." "Yellowstone Park Association" emblazoned another pennant at one time. Two of the eight flagpoles were removed around 1927. Another flagpole was apparently removed in 1954, leaving five flagpoles marking the Inn's summit. Bellman Gary Gebert raised a "Yellowstone Park Company" pennant on the fifth flagpole during his tenure (1969-1980). More recently, the fifth pole has been designated for special use. It was last used in 2000 to fly an employee-signed banner as a heartfelt memorial for Inn employee Sara Hulphers. Today, the United States flag

and the three state flags proudly fly from the Inn's peak.[6]

A naval spotlight was erected on the widow's walk in the hotel's first year to highlight night-time displays of Old Faithful Geyser, garbage-feeding bears, or occasionally "rotten loggers," a term given to young sweethearts. Another spotlight was added to this skyline platform around 1910. These "theatrical" spotlights were removed in 1948.[7] The Inn's manager at that time stopped access to the upper reaches of the Inn and the widow's walk because of safety concerns. Even after the spotlights no longer crowned the Inn, visitors could experience a nightly illumination of the famous geyser. The first eruption after 9 pm—through at least the 1950s—was highlighted courtesy of a spotlight tucked into a grove of trees near the end of the East Wing, operated by the National Park Service.[8]

Reamer cleverly positioned Old Faithful Inn so visitors could enjoy a grand view of Old Faithful Geyser upon arrival, but this view wasn't available to guests once inside. Perhaps he was encouraging guests to wander outdoors and engage in the richer pedestrian pilgrimage needed for true appreciation of the geyser basin.[9]

Walk beneath the porte cochere—the original stage way—and imagine wealthy customers

Long time park employee Tom Robertson unfurling Old Glory on top of Old Faithful Inn on an early morning in June 1988. Like many Yellowstone employees, Tom has worked a wide variety of jobs in the interest of staying in the park. According to Tom, however, his favorite job of all was working as a bellman in the Inn. For him, nothing has been better than working in the lobby of the great building and living in Bats Alley, a hallway on the west side of the lobby that for many years has served as living quarters for Old Faithful Inn bellhops.
(Photo ©Jeff Henry)

gingerly disembarking from their horse-drawn buggies or stagecoaches dressed in clothes of the early 1900s. Beneath lengthy linen "dusters" (coats rented to protect their fine clothing from fine dust kicked up by horses, wheels and wind), women wore starched white blouses adorned with brooches, long skirts, hats and gloves, while men donned hats and handsome three-piece suits complete with pocket watches.[10]

Many of these tired, dusty folks were accustomed to fine hotels of the east and were no doubt ready for a little pampering. Their journey to the world's first national park was often not easy or convenient. Early roads were atrocious: steep grades were par, and roads were deeply rutted and sported occasional tree stumps. Water was sprinkled on the roads to keep them "in good order and free from dust."[11]

Ornamental wrought-iron lamps suspended from the ceiling of the porte cochere cheerfully illuminated the Old Faithful Inn entrance in 1904 and still do today. Their glow must have been a welcome sight to weary travelers, hinting at the warmth and comfort to be found inside.[12]

A naval searchlight was installed on the roof of the Inn during its first year of operation. The light was used, of course, to illuminate nighttime eruptions of Old Faithful Geyser. Some find irony that it was a naval searchlight that was installed on top of the widow's walk, an element with similarly maritime associations. A second light was added sometime around 1910. Both were removed from the Inn in 1948. The National Park Service, however, continued to illuminate the first eruption of Old Faithful after 9 pm until sometime in the 1950s. The park service's light was in a grove of trees somewhere near the end of the East Wing, probably on or near the site of the existing Visitor Center. *(Photo courtesy Haynes Foundation Collection, Montana Historical Society, Helena, Montana)*

Like a sentinel guarding the valley below, the grand old hotel stands watch over Mother Nature's wild, weird and wonderful.

CHAPTER NINE

Old Faithful Inn Welcomes its Guests

"I am glad to see you! Walk right in! Make yourself at home."

—LARRY MATHEWS,

FIRST MANAGER OF OLD FAITHFUL INN, 1904[1]

WHEN OLD FAITHFUL INN OPENED in late spring of 1904, its Upper Geyser Basin location delighted guests immediately, but the comfort and security afforded visitors within the wilds of Yellowstone was a positive too. The heavy plank double door suggested the rustic grandeur within—its bold red hue the universal color of welcome. Strapped in heavy wrought iron and bejeweled with over a hundred iron studs, these 6½' by 7' doors were supported by heavy iron hinges and fitted with iron lock, key and peephole grill—all hand-forged by Colpitts and other blacksmiths under the auspices of Reamer. The fifteen inch key and lock were said to weigh a hefty twenty-five pounds. This massive hardware conjured up images of secure medieval castles while Reamer's practical use of local logs was reminiscent to some of a frontier fort.[2]

On the inside of the double door, there is a wrought-iron apparatus: an old-fashioned coil spring and round clapper that once served as a door bell for tardy tourists. Legend has it the Inn was locked to all intruders

Larry Mathews, the first manager of Old Faithful Inn. Erstwhile operator of a number of lunch stations around Yellowstone, Mathews spent one summer at the Inn, presiding over the building during its inaugural season in 1904. (Photo courtesy Montana Historical Society, Helena, Montana)

51

in its early days, but if you were a late-arriving registered guest, you merely had to pull the dangling cord that was on the outside of the door to ring the bell and gain admittance to the comforts within.[3]

The cavernous lobby, labeled the "main office" in Reamer's blue-print plans, stretches nearly seventy-seven feet to the ceiling's apex. Balconies with whimsical pine rails and supports encircle the second floor while the third floor balcony services only the lobby's north and east edge. More hand-hewn log stairs and catwalks ascend beyond the third floor and snake up to lofty platforms and a fanciful tiny house. Over one hundred steps transport guests from floor to zenith of this great room.[4]

Nestled under the northeast corner of the lobby's ceiling, Reamer and his workers built a little house, adorned with crooked limbs in keeping with the rest of the lobby. This little house has its own roof, hinged airy windows and door. The enchanting quality of the quaint house (some-times labeled the "Crow's Nest"), reminded yes-terday's visitors of a childhood tree house, real or imagined. Early day visitors could climb up to this jewel through the lobby's forested environs and peer down at goings-on far below. Musicians sometimes entertained from the lofty Crow's Nest and other balconies as guests celebrated and danced on balconies below.[5]

The Inn's lobby space could be overwhelming—making a person feel small and insignificant—but Reamer and Mrs. Child created a homey feel in the rough quirky architecture and the rustic comfortable furniture. Throughout the Inn, cozy ornamental nooks grounded the mas-sive space and invited visitors to settle in with a good book or conversation. Strategic lighting added to the pleasing allure of the Inn. Ingenious candlestick electric lights and candelabras lent light to the vast yet intimate space around the clock. During daylight hours or moonlit nights, a multitude of windows further illuminated the lobby from without.

Visitor Clifford P. Allen remembered his warm welcome by the illustrious Larry Mathews, first

manager of the Inn. He recalled Larry as an Irishman bedecked in his best hat, a Tipperary (skull cap), who made Allen and other guests feel welcome with his heavy brogue and hearty, warm greeting.

Allen recalled another colorful moment with the Inn's first manager. In 1904, church services were held one evening in the Old Faithful Inn's lobby. After repeatedly checking his timepiece, manager Mathews announced to the assembled worship-pers that Old Faithful was about to erupt. In response to the preacher asking for more time for closing hymn and benediction, Larry said, "You cannot have them[;] the Geezer waits for no mon [man]." And so, that was the end of the church service as everyone filed out to watch the geyser play under the illumination of the Inn's spotlights. According to Allen, "Old Faithful geyser came to time to the minute" and Larry was praised more than the preacher was![6]

Sitting in the lobby's southeast corner, is the behemoth 15½-foot eight-hearth fireplace crafted from 500 tons of native volcanic stone. Imagine how workers must have pried the gigantic boul-ders from their earthly resting spot and hefted them mightily into place, one atop the other as the monument climbed to soaring heights. The tapering fireplace stretches forty-two feet before pushing another forty feet beyond the roof. Its original exterior stack was of brick con-struction, sheathed with log cribbing similar to the chunky porch piers. Today, a self-supporting steel stack extends beyond the roof. The log cribbing is slated to be replaced in an upcoming restoration project.[7]

Closeup of hardware and slabbed logs on the inside of Old Faithful Inn front doors. Yellowstone Park in 1904 was only two decades or so removed from its days as a raw frontier. Indeed, only 26 years had passed since the last armed conflict in the park between whites and Native Americans. Genteel visitors from more civilized sectors of the country almost certainly were con-cerned about dangers real and imagined when they visited the park, especially when the gloom of night descended over the geyser basins. With these thoughts in mind, it is not surprising that Robert Reamer designed such stalwart doors for the front of his great building. It requires little imagina-tion to see the resem-blance of these doors to those of a frontier fort. It also is not surprising that these massive doors were locked securely at night in the early days of the Inn. *(Photo ©Jeff Henry)*

The fanciful Crow's Nest, situated high above the lobby floor. Musicians sometimes played in the Crow's Nest for the benefit of guests down below. *(Photo ©Jeff Henry)*

Early visitors warmed body and soul at the four large hearths circumventing the stone obelisk. Rocking chairs were offered guests within a sunken area encircling the fireplace, which helped create the inviting ambience of the Inn. Twenty-two years after the Inn opened, a concrete floor was poured around the fireplace area to raise it from its original recessed state. Before 1927, a one- or two-sided rail served to isolate guests from passersby in the cordoned area.[8]

During the restoration project of 2004-2006, the floor next to the fireplace will be restored to its original sunken level. Rails will once again separate wandering visitors from those cozying up to the fire's warmth.[9]

The comforting sounds and smells of fresh popcorn popping often filled the lobby in the hotel's infancy—a welcome treat after a long day of geyser gazing. A railroad historian wrote in 1905:

Fires of big logs are kept going constantly in the large fireplaces, and every evening a massive specially-made, swinging corn popper is brought into play and the guests regaled with popcorn passed around in a large dishpan.

This after-dinner custom of heaping up a "great snow bank of popcorn" continued at least through 1914. The authentic wrought-iron popper still hangs from the fireplace wall today. Absent is the hollowed-out knot with a hinged lid that used to house a handy shaker of salt.[10]

The Old Faithful Inn's famous clock, positioned against the north face of the massive stone chimney. *(Photo ©Jeff Henry)*

Adorning the front of the fireplace, the twenty foot long clock designed by Reamer and hammered out by Colpitts still evokes curiosity and respect one hundred years later by all who pause to appreciate its proportions. In September of 2000, Dave Berghold, Mike Kovavich and Dick Dysart restored this failing icon. Before they created its new endless rewind system, bellhops cautiously clambered out on Colpitts's narrow iron scaffolding—nearly three flights up—to wind the clock, putting weekly trust in Colpitts.

The five foot clock face with eighteen inch red Roman numerals, fourteen foot pendulum with copper disk, and wrought-iron counterweights and brackets are all original. The revived clock now has yard-long metal arms (replacing wooden ones) and new works. In wee hours of the morning or late in the evening when most

folks are courting dreams, the loudest sound in Old Faithful Inn is the slow two-second rhythmic *tick tock,* helping to mark time in this timeless Inn.[11]

When the Upper Geyser Basin's grand hotel hosted its first guests in June 1904, a visitor could book a room with bath-down-the-hall for $4. (A century later, with inflation, this room would cost about $77.)[12] Guestrooms had an easy-going coziness—the rooms' walls and ceilings were wrapped in the warmth of rustic unfinished wood. Old House first-floor rooms had unpeeled log walls and ceilings, while upper story rooms had rough-sawn board paneling. Curtained windows were often cracked to admit fresh, mountain air and the whiff of geysers, reminding visitors they were in the world's first national park. Novel lighting, flowers in a vase, rugs, and simple furnishings made guests feel at home. Pegs for parasol, hat or cloak were usual room embel-lishments. Each room differed from the next in size and accents, and a few featured cushioned window seats.[13]

An operational bell call system connected guest rooms with bell staff until 1970.[14] Bellman Don Shaner recalls manning the lobby's bell desk; one bell was a call for service which could mean *anything.* (One guest summoned him because she was sure there was a ghost in her room. Shaner discovered that the hissing steam from the laundry pressing plant behind the Inn was the cause of the ghost-like sound.)[15] Two bells was a request for ice and three bells meant luggage porters were needed to haul bags from the rooms. Bell staff knew which room needed service because an arrow would trip on the bell board, indicating the room number when the bell rang.[16]

Just outside, bellmen lined up their luggage carts in "Pierre's Garden," the Old House concrete porch with iron-wrapped pine pillars, named after bellman and bell captain Pierre Martineau (1959-1970). Bellhops still called the porch "Pierre's Garden" in 2003. In 1959, Bellman Robert Mautino christened one of these carts, a

In the wee hours of the morning or late in the evening when most folks are courting dreams, the loudest sound in Old Faithful Inn is the slow two-second rhythmic *tick tock,* helping to mark time in this timeless Inn.

small four-wheeled luggage cart favored by bellman Don Shaner, the "Shane" cart. The "Shane" cart was still in service in 2003.[17]

By the beginning of the 2005 season, this fascinating bell call board will reside in a more favorable location near the registration desk. It will remain nonfunctional. The board offers a snapshot of day-to-day operations in the Inn's scrapbook of time.[18]

The Old Faithful Inn's 1904 opening season coincided with the St. Louis World's Fair. In August of that year, a picture of Old Faithful Inn was shipped to St. Louis, Missouri, where it was exhibited in the Montana building to promote trips to Wonderland. The exposition drew people from all over the world to the United States that summer. Hotel business was good in Yellowstone National Park that year too; forty percent of Child's clientele at Old Faithful Inn were international visitors.[19]

Most visitors seemed pleased with the debut of Old Faithful Inn and the opportunity to leisurely explore the Upper Geyser Basin that it afforded them. The Inn's opening season also satisfied stockholders. Its total gross earnings topped $45,000 that season, turning a much needed profit. Historically, hotel operations had been a losing prospect for the Northern Pacific Railroad's interests. Child, the Yellowstone Park Association, architect Reamer, his craftsmen, and of course, the employees and paying guests, all played important roles in the Inn's initial success.[20]

A female visitor enjoying herself by the window of Room 46 in the early days of the Inn.

The identity of these men is a mystery. They appear to be men of substantial position, perhaps either hotel company officials or perhaps simply well-to-do visitors. The man perched on the foundation behind the trio strongly resembles Harry Lloyd, an early day stage driver in Yellowstone. If so, Lloyd perhaps could have been assigned to transport the men around the park on whatever their business might have been. This photo was probably taken sometime before 1910.
(Photo courtesy Bessie Ferguson Collection, Harry Child II)

An old Detroit
Photographic Company
postcard showing the
fireplace and the interi-
or of the original din-
ing room. Note the
long carpet runner as
well as the tables set up
for family style dining.

8808. DINING ROOM, OLD FAITHFUL INN, YELLOWSTONE PARK.

28461 OLD FAITHFUL INN DINING ROOM, YELLOWSTONE PARK   HAYNES.

Old postcard shot of
the interior of Old
Faithful Inn dining
room addition of 1927.

CHAPTER TEN

The Charm of Old Faithful Inn

Dining, Dancing and More

*"We had such a jolly time dancing and singing on the second floor balcony
while corn was being popped below in the big fireplace."*

—MRS. EDWARD H. JOHNSON, GUEST 1905[1]

AFTER GUESTS MADE TREKS ROUND THE GEYSER BASIN alternately breathing in the thermal area's mal-odorous smells and Yellowstone's clean mountain air, they had earned their meals. Old Faithful Inn once had a bell poised atop the hotel that declared dinner one-quarter hour before sit-down time. Some guests lined up in front of the dining room door before the bell tolled, in anticipation of gastronomical delights to be found within. A Montana newspaper noted in 1914:

> *A bell-hop in white duck trousers and undertaker's gloves jumps a couple of feet off the floor and grabs hold of a rope dangling in front of the big open fire place. The bell rings!*

The relaxed atmosphere of Old Faithful Inn settles in after dark, like gently falling snow after winds that brought the storm.

The dining room doors were swung open and hungry guests hurried in "to secure another $5 meal for about 75 cents." The 1914 article sings high praises for Child's hotel company, its food and service. From the beginning, the full-service dining room has offered three square meals a day.[2]

Another old postcard view, this one of the interior of an upper floor guest room.

Before 1922, there was only one dining room—its tables could not seat all of the Inn's guests simultaneously. Annie Bucklee, a guest in August 1905, wrote in a letter to her mother:

I must not take much more time or I may not get any dinner[;] the bell is ringing now and the dining room only holds about ½ of the people in the hotel, so they have two sittings and they are 1 hour apart and after our ride we are quite hungry.[3]

Upon hearing the dinner bell, visitors scurried back to their rooms to freshen up before dinner. Fresh water was provided guests on copper-topped wash stands in their rooms. Tan-colored pitchers and bowls in a floral pattern resided on top of each wash stand, while matching chamber pots rested on the table's bottom shelf. Clean white towels and washcloths hung from the simple rod above.[4]

The original dining room formed half an octagon sixty-two feet in diameter; later additions would better serve its abundance of guests. The dining room decor was in keeping with that of the lobby's. It had rustic log walls, a copper and iron chandelier, candlestick electric lights, and a long patterned rug that led to the large stone fireplace at its southern end. Unlike the hotel lobby, the dining room had log scissor trusses that supported its ceiling. A log partition screened the swinging doors between kitchen and dining room, and is still in use today.[5]

Everyone ate communally or "family style" from two long tables artfully set with china of a blue willow pattern and sparkling silver. Brass and copper accessories completed the table. Ladies and gentlemen were suitably dressed in fashionable gowns, suits, and ties, a sharp contrast to today's casual attire. A few seats afforded a popular view of Old Faithful Geyser, but after 1913, the East Wing addition blocked that view.[6]

Staff printed daily menus in the basement of the Inn, through at least the 1950s. Food items were not priced a la carte. Luxurious "all-you-can-eat" meals were either included in the hotel's "American Plan," or they could opt for the "European Plan" and pay for meals individually. (Chefs christened their creative dishes with names that sound today like recipes from *Gourmet* magazine.) In the 1960s, the dining room used a standard a la carte menu card that listed the same eight entrees each night. Hotel managers and guests relied primarily on time-saving breakfast and lunch buffets.[7]

Menus from 1911 give mouth-watering clues about the Inn's fancy fare. Breakfast items included shredded wheat biscuit, fried Lake Trout Meuniere, German fried potatoes, and eggs: boiled, fried, shirred (baked), scrambled or an omelette. After a geyser basin stroll, lunch guests might have enjoyed tenderloin of beef pique, cauliflower in cream, mashed potatoes, and pineapple sherbet for dessert. Dinner was the day's final taste-bud tantalizer: roast leg of pork with stewed prunes, duchess potatoes and carrots a la'Vichy. These items represented a mere fraction of the menu's offerings. Would the Inn's guests have had room for a wedge of blackberry pie or ribbon layer cake?[8]

At your next meal here, dream about the Inn's early day diners; perch yourself on the very same chairs that people of the early 1900s used as they relished the Inn's savory selections.

A government inspection report of 1916 gives clues about the dining room, kitchen, and larder. In the dining room, discipline prevailed and service was prompt. Large iceboxes cooled by ammonia and brine held beef, pork, lamb, corned beef, ham and bacon, tongue, and brook trout. There was also a supply of canned goods, fresh vegetables, and fruits. A French Chef was in charge of a "competent crew." Meals in the opening season cost the company about 65 cents from larder to table.[9]

The 1916 report also mentioned the Old Faithful hotel as "very well managed by a woman with executive ability." A guest seconded the effectiveness of this manager but in more of a "heartfelt" way:

> *something so homelike in the care and attention to details which Mrs. Underwood, the manager of the Inn, gives to the entire place...Most of all, we disliked to say good-by to the woman who makes this...good time possible for every guest.*[10]

Evening meals were accompanied by the soothing sounds of a string quartet from the small gallery overlooking the dining room on the lobby's second floor balcony. Later ensembles changed to accomodate popular music. Seven musicians who played there in the mid-1920s wrote their names near the tiny balcony for posterity. In the 1960s, modern quartets also entertained guests from this balcony, keeping the tradition alive.[11]

After dinner, regular entertainment was arranged for guests' enjoyment or participation. Merriment sometimes included reading poetry or singing around the piano. An account of a "perfect climax to a perfect day" in the Inn's "friendly living room," mentioned guests "gathered about the piano [on] the balcony." They sang "the best loved songs of north and south and east and west."[12]

OLD FAITHFUL INN

Dinner

Cream of Tomato   Consomme in Tasse
     Salt Wafers   Melba Toast
Sweet Pickles   Radishes   Ripe Olives
Fried Filet of Sole with Tartar Sauce
Boiled Ham with Green Spinach
Broiled Sirloin Steak Maitre de Hotel
Compot of Rice with Fresh Fruit Sauce
Chicken Fricassee with Steamed Rice
Mashed Potatoes   Cauliflower au Gratin
Candied Sweet Potatoes   Carrots Saute in Butter
Sliced Tomatoes French Dressing
Heart of Lettuce Salad 1,000 Island Dressing
Rolls   French, Raisin, Rye, and Wheat Bread
Maple Cream Puffs Hot Mince Pie Melba Peaches
Table Apples Chocolate Ice Cream Assorted Cookies
American, Swiss or Cottage Cheese Crackers
Coffee   Postum   Tea   Milk   Iced Tea
          Cocoa   Demi Tasse
Old Faithful Inn   Sunday, August 31, 1930

Lectures by Ranger Naturalist on the Geysers history bears, etc., at Bear Feeding Grounds at 7:00 p. m.; at Museum at 8:15 p. m. Searchlight on Old Faithful Geyser Time announced in lobby.

Printed menu from Old Faithful Inn, dated August 31, 1930. A printing press in the Inn's basement printed daily menus through at least the 1950s.

Eleanor Hamilton Povah recalled her most memorable recollection of Old Faithful Inn:

> *My mother was a magnificent singer. There was a piano in the corner by the bar. Mom would sing with piano accompaniment, and fill the entire lobby with her rich, full and beautiful voice.*

According to Eleanor, her mother, May, gave up a career as a professional singer and entertained Inn guests as a hobby instead.[13]

When it was time to dance, early day rugs were rolled up and along with furniture, were pushed back to the periphery and the fun began. Musicians reportedly climbed to one of the mezzanines above or to the Inn's lofty playhouse to send notes floating through the Inn's lovely space to dancers below. The Fred Gebert Orchestra played from the elevated balcony along the Inn's front wall from 1928-1932. This required musicians to hike with instruments in tow nearly to the Crow's Nest. The group would occasionally play for private dances in the dining room.[14]

Dancing was customary six nights a week at Old Faithful Inn and later at Old Faithful Lodge, built in the mid-1920s. By 1937 most dances were held at the Lodge recreation hall. However, national sorority conventions were occasionally held in the Inn. On these occasions, the lobby filled with lovely girls dressed in formal gowns ready to dance. Small musical ensembles continued to give concerts in the Inn on Sunday nights, on an elevated platform in the southwest corner of the lobby through at least the 1930s. A flyer that advertised guest services for the Inn mentioned "occasional evening entertainment" in 1967.[15]

The Yellowstone Park Company moved an organ into the lobby about 1940. William Fitzpatrick played the organ that year. A Haynes photograph of Fitzpatrick shows a small, rustic platform—barely large enough for the organ and a scooted-out bench. Fitzpatrick entertained guests just outside the entrance doors of the original Bear Pit (cocktail lounge).[16] Judith Turck, a native Montanan, played the organ at Old Faithful Inn and Canyon Hotel in the 1950s. A bellman remembered Turck: "She had red hair, wore four to five inch heels and pumped the organ pedals with enthusiasm!" Judith played

guest-requested school fight songs and "songs to go to sleep to," and during the occasional dance held in the lobby, some bellmen requested waltzes. Employees could attend if they "dressed up."[17] Another Montana native, Jeannie Shadoan Keeter, played the organ in the mid-1960s. During dinner, she played in the southeast corner of the original dining room. Waiter Charles "Moon" Mullins remembered Jeannie turning scarlet when "all those dudes would drop their forks and give total attention to her version of [Temptation]." After the meal, she wheeled her organ into the Bear Pit bar and played until about midnight.[18]

In recent years, a pianist has entertained guests from the second floor balcony during dinner. George Sanborn has played "classical music or popular tunes people are likely to know" since 1992. He remembers that a lot of nice people from all over the world have paused at his piano—singers, a flutist, a concert violinist, a concert pianist—but a professional vocalist from Belgium stands out. Sanborn recalls: "She hit a high note. The Inn vibrated and caused everyone in the Inn to stop whatever they were doing. People wondered aloud 'what happened.'"[19]

Guests of Old Faithful Inn swaying to the music on a long ago evening, probably in the 1930s. *(Photo courtesy Haynes Foundation Collection, Montana Historical Society, Helena, Montana)*

Leather-burning artist Jim Cole working on a piece in the lobby in 1988. Jim was artist in residence at the Inn from 1985 through 1994. *(Photo ©Jeff Henry)*

Montana native Jim Cole pleased guests with double talents at the Inn. An artist in residence there for ten years, Jim created works of art by burning leather with a hot iron. Blessed with a beautiful voice that can literally fill every nook and cranny of the cavernous lobby without amplification, Cole switched talents in the evening and entertained guests with selections from Broadway musicals and western medleys from 1989-1994.[20]

In 2003, the first artist-in-residence since Cole, James Reed offered watercolor paintings in the northeast corner of the Inn's entrance area. Besides paintings of the Inn and park wildlife, many of his images depicted a firefighting theme.[21]

The Bear Pit lounge was home to various musical acts over time. Yellowstone Park Company employees by day and folk musicians by night, "The Windy Hill Singers" and "The Four of Us" entertained lounge guests twice weekly in the 1960s. Both groups later recorded albums. In 1979, Billy Abel entertained Bear Pit guests with regular evening performances. Exceptionally talented, he played guitar and sang country-western songs. A one-man-band nicknamed "Clyde the Slide" provided dance music one year later. Space was set aside for a modest dance floor opposite the bar in the Bear Pit.[22]

About three dozen singing waitresses and waiters in the 1960s added "vocal spice" to meals enjoyed by Old Faithful Inn diners. They performed each evening, once before dinner and again at 8:00 p.m. "Dixie" and "Yankee Doodle" were crowd favorites, but the pastel-uniformed group also performed folk music with guitar accompaniment. In 1967, they were the featured lunch-time entertainment for attendees of the Western States Governors' Conference.[23]

"Muzak" was popular across the nation by the 1950s and reached the Inn by 1959. Piped into the lobby's speakers, this soft music persisted there on a regular basis through at least the mid-1970s. Today this music system is still used occasionally.[24]

Early on, Old Faithful Inn was a full-service hotel. It offered services beyond the simple necessities of food, water, and shelter. The front desk naturally made reservations for hotels and concessionaire tours, but mail, laundry, and tailor services were also available. A guest in need of libation could find stool and bartender in the Inn's nether regions from the beginning (at least until prohibition). By 1912, and perhaps earlier, the Inn offered other luxuries to its patrons, services they were accustomed to finding in the East's grand hotels. For the guest who was infirm, there was a dispensary and nurse to help. A guest in need of a trim could get a haircut in the barber shop. "Saddle horses, divided skirts and leggings" were also "for hire." A visitor could communicate by telegram around the world or by telephone within the park. By 1916, a beauty shop was mentioned. Top-shelf cigars, newspapers, and a shoeshine stand were also available.[25]

In 1900, a Mammoth hotel newsstand inventory listed items for sale—probably similar to those offered guests when Old Faithful Inn opened. They included: playing cards, blue-colored spectacles, bottled sand, Jamaica[n] Ginger (Extract), Bromo Seltzer, chewing gum, and various curios: watch charms, beads, baskets, idols, arrow points, thermometers, and agate quartz.[26]

F.J. Haynes operated the only photography concession in Yellowstone National Park from 1884-1916. His Log Cabin Studio was built between the Inn and Castle Geyser and remained there until 1932. In Old Faithful Inn's early days, Haynes offered photographs, film and souvenirs near the entrance of the present-day gift shop,

A BELLHOP'S DREAM REALIZED

After World War II, Warren Ost came to the Old Faithful Inn as a college student. He grew up in Minnesota, and following a long family tradition, boarded a train for Yellowstone National Park and his summer job. Ost was employed as a bellhop for three seasons at the Inn. According to his wife Nancy, "he was thrilled to go up on the Inn's roof and raise the flag." But that was not all that bellhop Ost raised.

Ost realized that spiritual guidance in the park was virtually absent and recognized the opportunity to develop and offer some religious focus for college students. With cooperation from the National Park Service and the National Council of Churches, Ost began a Christian Ministry program in Yellowstone National Park in 1951. He elevated the program to "A Christian Ministry in National Parks," and served as its first director one year later.

Ost devoted his life to a career with "A Christian Ministry in National Parks." Today, as a result of his work, about 300 seminary students are placed in 65 national parks, national forests, and resort areas around the country. Among other jobs, they work as bell-men, waiters, and service station attendants. On Sundays, they offer church services in some of the world's most beautiful places. And it all began at Old Faithful Inn.

In Yellowstone, 45 students offer inter-denominational worship services in campgrounds, lodges and hotels. The Old Faithful area typically has a team of around ten students. Church services are held at 8:00 and 11:00 Sunday morning on the Old Faithful Inn's porte cochere balcony. Bird song and geyser gush blend sweetly with human voices during the worship services.[1]

as there was no real "gift shop." (One guest room was sacrificed c.1915 to create a small "art shop.") His son, Jack E. Haynes, took over the photo business in 1917 and operated it until his death in 1962. The Haynes counter of offerings moved to the southwest corner of the Inn for four years beginning in 1923.[27]

In 1927, a gift shop was created from five more guestrooms—further augmented by the outward extension of the north wall. The Haynes photo shop relocated to the gift shop; its counter was along the window. As a Haynes employee in the late 1930s, Allen Crawford was expected to wear three-piece suits and drew a good wage—$30/month. His pet peeve was impatient customers that would clank coins on his glass counter.

Jack Haynes cut a striking figure with his tall good looks and cut-off cigar protruding from his pipe. A successful entrepreneur with a sense of humor, Jack would strut into Old Faithful Inn and ask his employees in a loud voice for a *Haynes Guide*. For half a century, Jack published yearly editions of the *Haynes Guides*—a visitor "must have" for touring the park. His extensive park knowledge earned Jack the charismatic title "Mr. Yellowstone." Dignitaries and statesmen were often his guests; they stayed at the Inn.[28]

For many years, the Inn's Indian Gift Shop was located in the lobby's northwest corner, beyond the current gift shop. (The Indian gift shop was moved to the back of the gift shop in 1988.) In the early 1960s, the shop was operated as a separate concession. The Yellowstone Park

Another photo from the Bessie Ferguson collection, this one showing an unknown cook posing outside the Inn, brandishing sausages in one hand and a pitcher in the other. He possibly could have been a coworker of Bessie's, as she was known to have done food service work during other times in her Yellowstone career. *(Photo courtesy Bessie Ferguson Collection, Harry Child II)*

Company took over its management in 1964. Company buyers attended shows during the off-season to purchase merchandise for the Indian Gift Shop.[29]

In the late 1970s, the Gallup Indian Trading Company became the exclusive supplier for the Inn's Indian Gift Shop. John Kennedy managed the inventory for his family's company and remarked,

I saw the National Park Service as a sanctuary for authentic American Indian goods. I knew that every person coming to Yellowstone would enter Old Faithful Inn so I set out to develop a premier shop.

He worked closely with Evelyn Zimmerer, manager of the Indian Gift Shop from 1964 through 1986. Together, they artfully displayed beautiful Indian pawn jewelry, baskets, rugs, pottery, beadwork, and crafts, all representing various tribes. Kennedy remembered Zimmerer's enthusiasm and noteworthy skill of "selling high-ticket items," including fine Navajo rugs and $8000 black earthenware "Maria" pots.[30]

Today, Native American-made items in the gift shop are purchased or consigned through several vendors. Pawn jewelry is obtained through one vendor who works directly with artists on the reservations.[31]

For many visitors today, the relaxed atmosphere of Old Faithful Inn settles in after dark, like gently falling snow after winds that brought the storm. There are no more bustling crowds scurrying in and out with cameras and ice cream. Peaceful comfort floats over the Inn's guests like a warm blanket. During those last daylight hours at Old Faithful Inn, it is joyful to contentedly read, play a game, or engage in conversation with friends or family while sipping on a beverage from the Espresso Cart or Mezzanine Bar. As the Inn of long ago kept out the unpredictable wilds of Yellowstone, in the 21st century it shields people from their stressful lives, helping to build precious and magical memories for them to hold dear.

> The Inn shields people from their stressful lives, helping to build precious and magical memories for them to hold dear.

(Photo ©Jeff Henry)

Outside of East Wing.

(Photo ©Jeff Henry)

Old Faithful Inn Historic Renovations

"I discussed these additions briefly with Judge Edwards...
He said the time will come when this original unit of the Inn [Old House] will have to be scrapped
and its reconstruction then would have to be along the more practical lines of the additions."

—STEPHEN MATHER, 1927[1]

NEARLY 14,000 PEOPLE VISITED YELLOWSTONE when the Inn opened in 1904, but over the next ten years, their numbers pushed upward to an average of 21,500 visitors annually.[2] The railroads were bringing more and more people to Yellowstone and to respond to this increased visitation, the Yellowstone Park Association under Harry Child's leadership planned an annex to the Inn. Once again, Child borrowed money ($100,000) from the Northern Pacific Railroad to accomplish this task.

Child commissioned "Yellowstone Architect" Reamer to design a three-story east wing addition to Old Faithful Inn. Apparently, Reamer decided that the unique architectural statement of the old house was not to be contested, so the East Wing was designed with a flat roof. Double hung windows gave the addition a symmetrical appearance. Like the Old House, it had a native stone-veneered foundation with exterior walls sheathed in cedar shingles, and its corners were finished by log cribbing. But the rooms' interior walls' treatment was lath and plaster and lacked the romance of the Old House's rough sawn plank or half-log walls. The East Wing was attached to the Old House by a two-story passageway, its top floor a breezeway.[3]

Now an even more imposing guardian of the geysers and keeper of guests, Old Faithful Inn boasted a length of approximately 836 feet and offered a total of about 340 rooms.

Like the construction of the Old House a decade earlier, the project persisted throughout the winter of 1913-1914. With the completion of the East Wing, the Inn could offer 100 additional rooms for rent by next season's commencement. Bernard O. "Pete" Hallin served as construction foreman for the new East Wing. His crew lived behind the hotel in tent cabins made of dimensional lumber frames topped with canvas. Christened "Poverty Row" in later years, these rough accommodations served workmen during future projects as well.[4]

For two seasons beginning in 1920, waitresses served hungry guests under a makeshift canvas-roof addition south of the original dining room. Reamer completed the much-needed dining room addition in 1921-1922. This new dining area was connected to the old by converting two exterior windows of the original dining room to door-ways. Five years later, Reamer built yet another dining addition along the eastern flank of the original dining area. The original dining room's eastern wall was removed except for its supports. For thirty-five years, the Inn had a three-room dining area. This multi-sided addition was converted in 1962 to today's Bear Pit lounge.[5]

Today, the registration desk sits in the lobby's northeast corner, relocated in 1923 from its original southwest location, to decrease congestion in front of the dining room. Also in that year, a bell desk was installed opposite the registration desk. Both desks eliminated Old House guestrooms to enlarge the lobby space and better serve the visitor. Because of the missing guestroom wall, stair-

case posts and rail opposite the bell desk were added. Before 2004, the activity desk in the lobby's southwest corner was the original registration desk. After the 2004 restoration project, a new volcanic rock counter will occupy that space and serve as a hostess stand instead.[6]

The sidewalk immediately outside the front door, under the Inn's porte cochere, was originally the drive-through area. To enlarge the lobby in 1927, under Reamer's direction, the red entrance door and its wall with large plate glass windows were pushed out approximately thirty feet. Plate glass windows were added to the end walls, flooding the one-story-high entrance area with additional natural light. Five guestrooms' exterior walls were also removed and extended outward, creating space for the Inn's present gift shop. The original cribbed supports were then inside the lobby and were replaced by stout timber columns.

Plaque just inside front door of Old Faithful Inn. (Photo ©Jeff Henry)

Visitors today are greeted with a plaque just a few feet inside the door declaring that Old Faithful Inn was established as a National Historic Landmark in 1987. The plaque marks the original exterior wall's location.[7]

A breezy veranda was fashioned above the porch extension in 1927 and quickly became a popular place for geyser gazers. This stands in contrast to what some historians and architects guess Reamer's original intent was: to keep Inn and

geyser basin somewhat separate. Accessible from the second floor balcony, this veranda allows visitors to anticipate Old Faithful Geyser from the engraved, long, wooden benches. In very early morning, the veranda's sounds and sights tantalize the senses—nature's gifts. Chickadee songs, robin chirps, and the swish of swallows swooping between the tepee-like cross logs of the third floor dormers, can all be heard in concert against the geyser basin's steaming resonance, like a musical ensemble with background continuo.[8]

Old Faithful Inn underwent colossal changes in 1927 and 1928. Besides the lobby enlargement, open-air veranda, and east dining room projects, Child requisitioned Reamer to design a west wing addition to the Inn, again in response to increased park visitation and railroad pressure. As with the East Wing, Reamer proposed a flat roof design for practicality. Once again, he did not want the new annex to compete with the presence of the Old House.[9]

Park officials balked at his design; the proposed West Wing was visible simultaneously with the Old House to arriving tourists. They didn't want the original building's towering impact diluted by the more practical flat roof design of the new wing. Letters and telegrams flew among park headquarters in Mammoth, the National Park Service in Washington, D.C.,

and Reamer's Seattle office in June 1927. In regard to what he considered unacceptable design changes proposed by officials, Reamer wrote Child:

> I told you in my wire that I was as much interested in the appearance of Old Faithful Inn as the Government, and I will go further, and say it means a lot more to me...I hope that you will pardon me if I write rather feelingly about Old Faithful, but it was my first hotel, Child, and I am a bit sentimental about it.

After the sparks of heated discussion blinked out, Reamer's original design was given the green light. Like the East Wing, it would have cedar shingles covering its exterior and a flat tar roof, but the pitch of the mansard roof's overhang would be steeper and sport a series of small dormers. West Wing interior walls were of wall board unlike the East Wing room's lath and plaster. The four-story West Wing was connected to the Old House by an enclosed two-story lobby space.[10]

The West Wing was not built in winter, unlike the creation of the first two sections of the Inn. Construction of the expansive, four-story, Y-shaped West Wing began in late June 1927 and was complete by the season's end, adding 150 rooms with 95 baths to Old Faithful Inn's ability

Closeup of etching done by wood eating insects on post near dining room overlook. (Photo ©Jeff Henry)

bighorn sheep waiter, a pelican guest, and bears as bartender, wait staff, musicians, and customers. The Bear Pit served libations and featured light-breakfast and buffet-sandwich selections.[12]

When the Bear Pit was relocated to the east dining room in 1962, these wood panels were removed, stored and forgotten. Thankfully, architect Andy Beck and his restoration project of the 1980s unearthed the panels and brought five of them back to life—they now reside in their rightful home. Visitors today can relax and enjoy sandwiches and snacks while studying the craftsmanship of these wooden works of art in the Inn's snack shop, the Pony Express—the former Beguiling Bear Pit lounge.[13]

In the Inn's early days, the bark of the lobby's lodgepole pine forest was intact, giving it an even more "woodsy" feeling than today. In 1940, the bark was removed; the local legend was that bark peelings created a foot deep "carpet" on the lobby floor! When the logs were debarked to reduce a potential fire hazard or according to one source, because "too many guests were complaining that the rough logs were snagging their suits and the housekeepers were complaining about how hard it was to dust them," intricate lacy artwork was revealed. These whimsical tracings of one of Yellowstone National Park's small, unsung creatures—the pine bark beetle—were fine examples of Mother Nature's artwork. Some of the logs exhibited larger furrows tunneled into the wood, the product of wood borers—insects that work away beneath the bark unseen until the log is peeled. In 1971, all woodwork in the cavernous lobby was cleaned with compressed air and meticulously coated with protective varnish.[14]

to please its customers. Now an even more imposing guardian of the geysers and keeper of guests, Old Faithful Inn boasted an outside length of approximately 836 feet and offered a total of about 340 rooms. Child obtained loans from four railroads for the $210,000 project.[11]

The railroads were financially faithful to Child's ventures, because those projects served them well. The "Yellowstone Architect" was also faithful to Child's requests. Reamer returned again and again to Old Faithful Inn to do additions and renovations. Reamer's last project for the Inn, the Beguiling Bear Pit cocktail lounge (now the Pony Express Snack Shop) was sandwiched between the kitchen and the western edge of the lobby. Its creation was prompted by the National Park Service's decision to end an eighteen year hiatus on liquor sales three years after prohibition was lifted nationally in 1933. Reamer commissioned Chicago cartoonist Walter Oehrle to design and etch Douglas fir panels as wall decorations using a bruin theme. These intricately carved cartoons featured a dancing moose, a

Guests today can melt into the Inn's timelessness and indulge in self-pampering by using one of two original public bathrooms in the east wing of the Old House. Paved in petite black and white tile, the rooms showcase enameled cast-iron accoutrements: claw foot tubs and large sinks with back splash. A woven slat table rounds out the antiquated ensemble. Eight Old House rooms have private baths (as they did in 1904) and still utilize old-fashioned water closets with wall-mounted tanks. One has a copper-lined wooden tank, and the rest are porcelain.[15]

Today, in keeping with an Old House tradition, most guests use baths "down-the-hall" as they did when the Inn first opened. The second and third floors of each wing have complete bathrooms: showers, sinks and toilets. There is only one shower on the first floor, located in the east wing. Today, the privilege of a bath or shower is included in the price of a room. (The Inn's first guests had to pay fifty cents for cleanliness). While that may not seem like much, half a dollar in 1904 is just shy of a ten dollar bill a century later![16]

The majority of guests in the East Wing also used bathrooms "down the hall." Those rooms were not outfitted with bathrooms until 1967. Guestrooms in the Old House and the East Wing were updated with sinks, replacing the old-fashioned pitchers and bowls in 1924. Public restrooms probably became more necessary after World War II, when Old Faithful Inn itself became a destination. In an attempt to provide more public restrooms, the park superintendent approved pay toilets for the Inn in 1947.

Initially "flushed" by the National Park Service, the following March "three pay toilets in the men's public washroom and five pay toilets in the women's public washroom" were authorized by the NPS director. One free toilet remained available in each restroom. Auditor Jo Ann Hillard remembered collecting nickels from pay toilets in the 1960s. The women's restroom was on the first floor and the men's was in the basement.[17]

Today, in keeping with an Old House tradition, most guests use baths "down-the-hall" as they did when the Inn first opened.

Quaint clawfoot bathtub on second floor, east wing of Old House. *(Photo ©Jeff Henry)*

A 1927 sketch by Robert Reamer for the proposed West Wing of the Inn. Notice the steeply pitched roof, a feature that was not incorporated, of course, when the West Wing eventually was built in 1927. *(Drawing courtesy Haynes Foundation Collection, Montana Historical Society, Helena, Montana)*

GHOST ROOMS, GHOST STORIES

As guests' needs changed, Old Faithful Inn rooms were sacrificed. The Old House probably had 140 guest rooms originally. A few of these rooms likely housed female employees until the women's dormitory was built in 1922. Today, only 87 original Old House rooms are available for rent.

Where did they go? The Inn itself reveals clues of how the old rooms were transformed to other purposes. Guest room "ghost" walls and doors give clues of where original guest rooms were located. But with the 2004 restoration project, the lobby and second floor mezzanine floor will be replaced. As a result, the evidence will be forever erased from the floor's wooden memory. Colpitts's hand-forged iron room numbers also give hints to the mystery of missing rooms. Nearly all of them appear to have their original numbers. Doors with missing numbers can also give leads; the outline of their old numbers can sometimes be detected.

As the lobby expanded, the number of guest rooms diminished. When the registration desk moved from the southwest to the northeast corner of the lobby and the nearby bell desk was created, four rooms gave up their original purpose. The creation of the present-day gift shop consumed six rooms. One gift shop office door still exhibits its original room number. For a more roomy access to the second floor veranda and to increase the sitting area for the mezzanine bar, several rooms were consumed. However, to beef up the Inn's seismic stability, two walls of these original rooms will be rebuilt with the restoration project of 2004-2006, creating mezzanine partitions. When the East and West Wings were annexed to the Inn and with the creation of public bathrooms, even more Old House rooms relinquished their initial roles.[1]

There are "ghost" rooms in Old Faithful Inn, but do *ghosts* reside within its wooden walls? Stories of inexplicable phenomena circulate through the century-old Inn on occasion, but are they true? The most common tale is of a headless bride who wanders down from the Crow's Nest. Past Inn manager George Bornemann admits that he simply "made up the tale" for a story-seeking reporter. Tour guide Betty Hardy handles ghost questions this way, "Do you believe in ghosts?" If they say yes, then she says "they're here." If they say no, then she says "they're not here."[2]

Old Faithful Inn in the "ghostly" geothermal steam of early morning. *(Photo ©Jeff Henry)*

Tour guide Betty Hardy handles ghost questions this way, "Do you believe in ghosts?" If they say yes, then she says "they're here." If they say no, then she says "they're not here."

10767. STAGES AT OLD FAITHFUL INN, YELLOWSTONE PARK.

1906 postcard view of porte cochere of the Inn.

CHAPTER TWELVE

Recreation and Resources Around the Inn

"The challenge lies not in combating such change,
but in learning to regulate it so that the environment suffers the least possible damage."

—RICHARD BARTLETT, HISTORIAN, 1985[1]

R ESOURCE USE IN YELLOWSTONE NATIONAL PARK has changed dramatically over time. Park managers have learned the importance of balancing resource protection with visitor enjoyment. But in Yellowstone's early days resource use favored visitor impulse and was not necessarily kind to the resource. Park rules that protected animals were not spelled out specifically until Congress passed the Lacey Act in 1894. Before that, fines could not be legally imposed if wildlife was abused or hunted.[2]

But regardless of Yellowstone's rules, visitors often meandered wherever they would, sometimes encouraged by colorful stagecoach drivers or tour leaders. It was not uncommon in Yellowstone National Park's early years for tourists to wander to the brink of, or even bathe in the thermal features. The non-soporific effect of soap on geysers was learned by 1885, practiced by guides and tourists, though frowned upon by the Army. (Company M of the United States Calvary was first stationed in the park in 1886 and

Some folks bottled up thermal water or took home vials of colorful mud—a far cry from today's "take only memories, leave only footprints" philosophy.

20136. HANDKERCHIEF POOL, YELLOWSTONE PARK.   HAYNES-PHOTO.

Early visitors clustered around Handkerchief Pool. The pool was named for its curious ability to swallow handkerchiefs, then regurgitate them a short while later in a laundered condition. Unfortunately, such abuse of the pool may have contributed to its demise. The sidewalk around the pool has since been removed.

stayed in their protective role until 1918.) Visitors carted home pieces of mineral deposits that ringed hot spring pools or purchased souvenirs that had been encrusted with the same. Some bottled up thermal water or took home vials of colorful mud—a far cry from today's "take only memories, leave only footprints" philosophy.[3]

Handkerchief Pool at nearby Black Sand Basin was a popular side trip for early day Inn guests. It was supposedly named in the early 20th century because ladies' linens were tossed in dirty and came out clean, to be fished out with a stick. People continued to throw objects into the pool and eventually its plumbing clogged. Even after diligent cleaning, Handkerchief Pool was never the same.[4]

The Upper Geyser Basin's Morning Glory Pool suffered a similar fate. Various forms of garbage were thrown into the feature's vibrant pool and its delicately scalloped edge was vandalized and carried away by visitors. Since the main road was routed away from this feature and Old Faithful Inn in 1972, Morning Glory Pool has healed somewhat after years of abuse. Park Service regulations wisely forbid throwing anything into thermal features to preserve plumbing, performance and natural beauty, and only allow photographs and memories to leave the park.[5]

Solitary Spring, a thermal feature tucked in the forest above Old Faithful Geyser, also suffered

from visitor use, but of a different nature. Henry P. Brothers proposed the building of a swimming pool at the Upper Geyser Basin. Acting Superintendent Lloyd Brett selected the site (on the thermal plain northwest of the Inn) and by July 1, 1915, more than one hundred swimmers could enjoy water piped downhill from Solitary Spring. (This spring is now known as Solitary Geyser—its performance was altered by plumbing water to the swimming pool.) For a dollar, twice the pool rate, Inn guests and others could soak in Old Faithful Geyser Baths, a more private opportunity to enjoy the natural waters of the Upper Geyser Basin and shrug off sore traveling muscles.[6]

In 1934, Hamilton Stores purchased the business from Brothers and constructed a new pool. Twelve hundred trees were harvested for the log work and 280,000 gallons of water were piped from Solitary Spring. The new building had an unbelievable 147 dressing rooms, two pools of different temperatures, and a front balcony with sand porches amazingly hauled from the distant shores of Yellowstone Lake. Inn guests bathed in the pool's thermal waters for thirty-six years before the National Park Service's philosophy changed and the pool was razed in 1951. Managers no longer would tamper with natural features to provide visitors with recreation opportunities.[7]

Inn guests in the early days could fish in the Upper Geyser Basin's Firehole River while watching geysers spout. The *Acting Superintendent's Report* of 1907 required that "no one person shall catch more than twenty fish in one day" and did not distinguish between sport and native fish. Special permits were granted employees who fished for park hotel dining rooms. On July 1, 1908, "the man at the Old Faithful Inn[,] who is the fisherman for the Hotel, caught fifty trout in the Firehole River." Today, a natural appreciation of the thermal basin—geyser gazing and wildlife watching—takes precedent over fishing the Upper Geyser Basin's waters.[8]

Before the mid-1920s, permanent tent camps were sprinkled throughout the park. The camps had everything for those who couldn't afford fancy hotels like Old Faithful Inn: tented dining halls, bathrooms, and lively campfires complete with dance, song, and conversation that differed from the more refined park hotels' entertainment. Their park tours were less expensive as well.

The most popular and established camp concession was the Wylie Permanent Camping Company. Their accommodations had wooden floors and half walls. Striped canvas finished the walls and roof with an informal "circus-like" flourish. In the Upper Geyser Basin, the Wylie Camp (1898-1916) was located on the hill west of Grotto Geyser. Within camp confines, street names illustrated their jovial nature: "Pleasant Way," "Rough Way," "No Way," "Tough Way," "Wrong Way," and "Right Way" to name a few.[9]

Campers occasionally visited the Inn. Two early 1900s diary entries related: "we dressed up... and went through Old Faithful Inn" and "after supper we put on our 'best togs' and went up to see the Old Faithful Inn." People not properly attired were probably not allowed admittance.[10] One evening, however, a "delegation" of Inn guests strode to a nearby camp and invited a group of unkempt musicians to play in the hotel lobby. The musicians arrived in camp-stained khaki suits and gave apologies for their disheveled appearance. A solo violinist stepped forward and commenced to play. An Inn guest wrote c. 1913:

> *the notes came clear and sweet...their harmony filling the court...touching every heart...These beautiful sounds were accompanied by a geyser, ending in a subdued melody just as the vaporous waters sank into the crater of Old Faithful.*

The Inn's guests were spellbound and speechless as they watched the violinist "vanish in the darkness back to camp."[11]

On August 1, 1915, the first horseless carriage, a Model T Ford Runabout, officially entered Yellowstone National Park—the last national park to give way to the motorized car. Automobile entrance fees varied between $5 and $15, based on carrying capacity. Depending upon park road conditions, speed limits varied from 8 to 20 miles per hour. Rules, strict timetables, and fines were imposed to keep the backfiring, odoriferous auto and sensitive horse apart. In 1916, automobiles shared the road somewhat precariously with horse-drawn carriages, taking turns for road privileges.[12]

A 1991 shot of park service personnel cleaning debris from Morning Glory Pool. The pumper trucks in the background had been used to lower the water level in the pool to facilitate cleaning. The man on the left is the late Rick Hutchinson, who indisputably knew more than anyone about Yellowstone's thermal features until his untimely death in an avalanche in 1997. *(Photo ©Jeff Henry)*

By 1916, one half of park visitors arrived by personal automobile, the preferred mode of transportation because of the independence they provided. Harry Child's stagecoaches were replaced by White Motor Company touring buses, forever ending an era. The fueling practices of park transportation changed from pitching hay to pumping gasoline. Old Faithful Inn's northern neighbor, the Fountain Hotel, was abandoned in 1917—obsolete because the automobile could access the more preferred destination of Old Faithful Inn in less time.[13]

More and more visitors were seeing Yellowstone "their way." Free automobile campgrounds sprang up out of necessity in 1916, with the Old Faithful area hosting one of four. By 1919, park superintendent Horace Albright recognized the growing need for modern campgrounds. One year later, campgrounds equipped with bathhouses and cooking spits were in service at Old Faithful and at Canyon. Lodges sprang up around the park after 1924 and though not as convenient as Lake Hotel or Old Faithful Inn, they were more affordable and served the "new" independent park visitor well. Park hotels now had serious competition from the popular lodges and automobile campgrounds. Though a completely different building, Old Faithful Lodge is often confused with Old Faithful Inn.[14]

Prior to World War II, Old Faithful Inn typically served well-to-do registered guests, for only they could afford railroad transportation. In 1904 a ticket from cities in Minnesota came with a $55 price tag—one hundred years later that amount inflated to $1700. The big double doors of Old Faithful Inn were locked in the evening, seemingly to keep nature's wonders, wildlife, and the less fortunate at bay. After World War II and perhaps to stimulate visitation, Old Faithful Inn itself became a park destination. To quote tour guide Ruth Quinn, "the Inn today is a public gathering place, regardless of income or conveyance" (or wardrobe)— a sharp contrast to its purpose in earlier years.[15]

> The fueling practices of park transportation changed from pitching hay to pumping gasoline.

Yellowstone National Park felt the effects of both World Wars and the Great Depression. It was more difficult for visitors to afford a trip to the park during these times and visitor services were sharply curtailed. Old Faithful Inn did not open in 1918 because of World War I. During World War II, the Inn remained closed for three seasons —1943 through 1945. Once the country's confidence was restored, however, park visitation rebounded beyond previous levels to set impressive new records in visitation. After World War II, in 1946, nearly 815,000 people visited Yellowstone National Park, more than twelve times the number of visitors just three years before.[16]

NO. 234. WYLIE CAMP AND UPPER BASIN—YELLOWSTONE PARK.

An overview of the Wylie tent camp on Wylie Hill, the small eminence to the west of Grotto Geyser.

PROPOSED ALTERATIONS OF
OLD FAITHFUL INN, YELLOWSTONE PARK, WYO.
R. C. REAMER, ARCHITECT

A circa 1927 pencil drawing of the front
of Inn by its designer Robert Reamer.
(Photo courtesy Haynes Foundation Collection,
Montana Historical Society, Helena, Montana)

CHAPTER THIRTEEN

Behind the Scenes

"In the rear of the hotel was a power house and a sawmill...
It had lately been engaged in cutting firewood for the house, of which hundreds of cords
were piled around. This is the only fuel to be had here."

—CLIFFORD P. ALLEN, GUEST, 1904[1]

T O OPERATE A HOTEL OF THE INN'S SIZE and to create its ambience, a multitude of unseen tasks occur daily. Let's take a look at behind-the-scenes happenings then and now—the nuts and bolts of Old Faithful Inn operations.

In 1913, a report disclosed "wood cut from park lands for building, repairs and fuel was done without payment to government." A contract between Yellowstone Park Hotel Company and a local logger in 1926 promised a whopping 1600 cords of wood for the Upper Geyser Basin, at a cost of $5.50/cord.[2]

Before World War II, the Inn's steam-powered boilers were fueled by lodgepole pine. The same tree species that comprised the Inn's walls also provided heat, hot water and electricity. Behind the Inn, enormous piles of cordwood sat ready for workers to load into railed cart. The carts efficiently hauled a cord (4'x 4'x 8') of wood to the boiler house with each roll.[3]

The building that housed these boilers still stands behind the Inn today, but its antiquated power sources have been replaced and updated. As a power source, pine wood eventually gave way to crude oil, black and thick as paint. Its acrid smoke rained down on any vehicles parked behind the Inn and ruined their paint jobs. Lighter fuel oil replaced crude oil in the late 1950s.[4]

"Steam engineer" Mike Parshall described the boilers as "steam

e Swift of a special
reservation crew
pplying stain to a
efurbished piece of
e Old Faithful Inn,
in the maintenance
rea behind the
nn, in 1995.
Photo ©Jeff Henry)

locomotives without wheels." Three immense side-by-side oil-burning boilers were kept under constant vigilance by employees or many of the Inn's systems would cease. (Today, the boilers are not manned around the clock; the system is computerized.) Powered by one *million* gallons of #5 fuel oil, the boilers powered the hotel's heating system, kitchen and laundry.[5]

The same tree species that comprised the Inn's walls also provided heat, hot water and electricity.

Boiler room employees worked in an unhealthy, dangerous and *hot* environment—kept at a constant and stifling temperature of 100 degrees Fahrenheit. Parshall recalled that "you could barely talk above the sound of the flames." As workmen lit the behemoth boilers with a diesel-soaked torch, a deafening "whoosh" engulfed the boiler room. Most of the workers smoked cigars and asbestos hung in tatters around a tangle of pipes.[6]

Parschall described the boiler room when he arrived: "it looked like a junk yard on fire." So, he and two other employees overhauled the boilers on their own time. The conscientious workmen noticed that the boilers needed a new coat of paint. Management had "red-penciled"

numerous requests for the required gallon of paint, so Parshall purchased the paint out of his own pocket. A reporter was searching for a woeful National Park Service budget story, but got wind of this personal sacrifice story instead. He photographed the employee painting the boiler and wrote the story. In early July 1981, the Wall Street Journal front-page headline read "More than a Gallon of Paint." The article caused "quite a stir" and the boiler man was relegated to a different park job the following season.[7]

Additional buildings and employees were needed to provide support services for the Inn: an engineer's cottage, carpenter and plumbing shops, and a chicken house, greenhouse, fire pump house, hose house, and laundry facilities. Other necessary infrastructure included: sewage and water systems, roads, utility tunnels, bridges, fences, pathways, a wood lot, and horse stables that could accommodate 125 head.[8]

A herd of around 45 milk cows kept Old Faithful Inn and its northern neighbor, the Fountain Hotel, supplied with fresh milk; their guests consumed 60 to 70 gallons per day in 1914. The herd was managed by three men near Lower Geyser Basin. Swan Lake Flat was pasture for cattle that supplied fresh beef to the park's hotels. There was a chicken house just south of the Inn which supplied fresh eggs for the dining room. In summer 1914, ice was manufactured by machine

The Old Faithful laundry, which cleaned linens for Inn guests through the 1985 season. The old laundry building still stands behind the Inn. It is now used as a recycling collection center. *(Photo courtesy Haynes Foundation Collection, Montana Historical Society, Helena, Montana)*

at the Inn for both geyser basin hotels. Seventy to eighty 100-pound cakes were made daily to keep perishables cold.[9]

The mercury dipped well below zero one September night in 1983. Pipes froze in the East Wing's unheated annex area, a fact that was revealed with a splash during the lunch hour. Until maintenance staff were located to turn the water off, bell staff filled 55 gallon drums with water, rotated full barrels out and empty ones in. (Today, maintenance men and women carry radios to deal with such emergencies.)[10]

For another type of emergency, a 1940s vintage Willy's Jeep fire truck sat behind the Inn for years. One afternoon each spring, a fire marshal trained bell and maintenance staff. Along with National Park Service personnel, they were expected to respond to area fires as needed. Bell staff lived on the fourth floor of the Old House's west wing (Bat's Alley), for a volunteer-firemen "presence." A shrill steam whistle on the top of the boiler room stack announced the fire, its location revealed by the number of times the whistle sounded.[11]

Old Faithful Inn had a laundry from its beginning. Initially small, it was enlarged in 1926 and a new facility was completed in 1958. It served the Inn through 1985. In later years, when not all locations had their own laundry facilities, laundry was trucked from other locations in the park to the Inn. (The laundry building still stands behind the Inn and is currently used as a staging area for recycling).[12]

"Bubble-queens," or laundry workers, kept the hotel in fresh linens and offered a three-day service to its guests. One-day service could be arranged for an "advanced rate." One million pieces of laundry were done each year at Old Faithful Inn alone. The tailor shop pressed and repaired clothes. A late 1920s chambermaid remembered a "laundry candy making party," after employees procured sugar and cream from the dining room. Nearly forty years later, Inn waitress Ginny Irvine remembered ingenious "popcorn parties in the laundry room using irons and jiffy pop." A laundry worker in the 1980s remembered regular afternoon breaks with supervisor-supplied watermelon. In 1982, a watermelon-shaped plaque commemorated that season's team—each seed held a laundry employee's name. Other plaques from past years' tributes to those that had washed and folded tons of sheets and towels hung proudly on the laundry walls.[13]

The number of Inn employees has varied through the years. A 1914 Old Faithful Inn report tallied 130 employees. Two later concessionaire pamphlets listed 250 people employed at the Inn after the West Wing completion. Today, about 350 people work at the Inn.[14]

Today, nearly thirty percent of the Inn's employees are involved with lodging aspects of the hotel. They help guests check in, make activity reservations, haul luggage, and keep rooms, lobby and other areas neat and clean. About half of the hotel's workers serve or prepare food or beverages.[15]

Bear Pit bartender Bob Adams ran a "tight ship" and ruled the bar for nearly three decades between 1947 and 1983. Management changed often and if they walked into the Bear Pit, Adams said he would tell them to "get out and stay out." Fortunately, he got along well with the "guests and kids that worked there." Adams met his wife

George
Bornemann,
known to some
as "Mr. Old
Faithful," who
lived and worked
in the Old Faithful
area for most of
the period between
1978 and 1998.
George's tenure
at Old Faithful
included two
seasons as manager
of Old Faithful
Inn, as well as a
great many
summers as a
bellman there.
(Photo ©Jeff Henry)

Irene at Old Faithful Inn—she waited tables in the dining room—and a generation later his son Jim, a waiter, met his wife at the Inn.[16]

Today, a handful of employees entertain and educate guests. A pianist plays during dinner from the second floor balcony. Three tour guides work at the Inn and four times throughout the day, a historical tour guide educates groups of curious guests and visitors. They parade through the celebrated hotel and pause at her many attractions. The front desk staff keeps one Old House guest room unoccupied for the tours' "show and tell." They cleverly reserve the historic tour's room under the auspicious name "Robert Reamer."[17]

Beginning about 1977 and lasting through the 1980s, park ranger interpreters gave "living history" presentations—dubbed the "chambermaid tour." Ranger Karen Boucher Selleck dressed the part in a blue muslin dress with pinafore apron, a white muslin cap and black tie shoes. Her feather duster completed the period costume. Tour participants were propelled back to a much earlier time— about 1915. Tamela Whittlesey gave tours in turn-of-the-century guest garb in the early 1990s for the concessionaire. Tour guide Betty Hardy remembered that tour participants were "most impressed by the lobby's height and that the Inn's logs once had bark on them."[18]

The rest of the employees are managers, work in the gift shop, maintain the hotel, or are truly "behind the scenes" people. These "invisible" personnel perform night security, do accounting, or serve employees rather than visitors.[19]

Initially, seasonal employees lived in the Old House, probably in upper floor rooms. "Bat's Alley," located at the very top of the Old House's west wing, has served as bell staff quarters for many years and continues in that purpose. In the mid-1960s bell staff lived in Bat's Alley only occasionally. "Rat's Alley," a name once given the Inn's basement rooms, served as cooks' housing and perhaps other employee quarters at one time. After 1928, the West Wing's basement rooms were probably employee rooms for a time. Early on, two bunkhouses and a winterkeeper house were erected behind the Inn to service staff.[20]

Dorm availability increased hotel profits by making more rooms available to the paying public. Behind the Inn, a men's dorm was constructed in 1913. In 1922, a women's dormitory was built. According to an old timer, the women's dorm's windows, doors, and oak staircase were salvaged from the Fountain Hotel. Interestingly, an Army era report noted the presence of *both* male and female dormitories in 1916: "every comfort was provided for: single beds, individual lockers, sani-

Tour guide Betty Hardy beginning a tour in front of the Old Faithful Inn fireplace.
(Photo ©Karen Reinhart)

tary toilets, plenty of bath tubs and a Chinaman doing the chamber work.[21]

A matron supervised the women's dorm. Her most important duty was to keep young men *out*. Not to be tricked, she cleverly smeared red lipstick on the dorm's fire escape rungs and caught sneaky culprits "red-handed!" In the 1970s, the dorm mother was nicknamed "Mama Bear."[22]

Another dorm, dubbed "Withering Heights" by Inn workers, was above the employee dining room. (Others called the dorm "W*u*thering Heights.") Past Inn manager George Bornemann recalled living there in 1979, the last year it housed employees. The north end of this L-shaped dorm currently houses mechanical and electrical equipment for the kitchen. It will be updated during the upcoming renovation project and perhaps someday will serve as housing once more.[23]

Employees today live in "Laurel" dorm (the original women's dorm, now coed) and in newer dorms and trailers in the housing area across the highway south of the Inn. Maintenance offices currently utilize the original E-shaped men's dorm located behind the Inn. Also in the hotel's backyard, the winterkeeper house still serves as a residence for the maintenance foreman.[24]

A hotel of the Inn's stature offers service and comfort with seemingly little effort—a sign of good management. But managers have encountered difficulties over the years. After World War II, many of the park's hotels and infrastructure suffered from cumulative disrepair. Heavy visitor use rained down on the park after the war and posed challenges for its managers.[25]

Today, the Historic Preservation Crew and maintenance personnel are watchdogs for potential structural troubles at Old Faithful Inn. Skilled workers have a long list of projects during every "off season" to ready the historic hostelry for next year's guests.

Before World War II, the hotel company hired professional wait staff, chefs, and managers. Southern resort employees followed the vacationing public north in summer, leaving the south's heat behind in the pre-air conditioning days. Orchestra members from large metropolitan areas traveled to the park as well. After the war, the park hired younger employees. Various railroads ran "savage specials" in spring and fall tailored for employees of Yellowstone hotels and lodges, photo shops, stores, and the National Park Service. The last non-stop Union Pacific employee train from Los Angeles, California to West Yellowstone was in 1956. After that, young

Foreman Fred Paulson pointing out a problem to be solved to Darren Kisor. Both men work on the Historic Preservation Crew in Yellowstone. The HPC, as it is known, tends to special maintenance requirements of all the old buildings in Yellowstone, but it seems that the Inn commands a disproportionate amount of their time. In this photo Kisor and Paulson were repairing one of the dormers on the front of the Inn that had been damaged during the winter of 1997, when a stupendous amount of snow accumulated in Yellowstone. Snow creep, a phenomenon that can be described as a very slow motion avalanche, had pulled this dormer loose from its attachment to the main facet of the Inn's roof. The Historic Preservation Crew successfully reattached it, as they had also done in 1996, when identical damage had occurred to the same dormer. *(Photo ©Jeff Henry)*

people rode freight trains—old cars with pot-bellied stoves—with stops and transfers en route before arriving at their park destination. A multitude of buses greeted trains in West Yellowstone and Gardiner. The fresh batch of recruits was then transported to various park locations.[26]

Occasionally Old Faithful Inn had personnel problems. Waitresses struck there twice: once in July of 1947 and again in August of 1962. In 1947, waitresses demanded (and received) free laundered uniforms. In 1962, nearly one hundred employees walked out of the dining room during the peak of the dinner hour. They complained about the firing of four waitresses and the company's lack of respect for employees. Satisfaction came two hours later when management promised to reinstate the four girls and fire a manager. Lodge wait staff could have saved the day, having finished their shift, but in the rebellious 1960s they were determined not to be "strike breakers."[27]

Chefs prepare and wait staff serve nearly 350,000 meals per season from the Old Faithful Inn dining room and the Pony Express. Over one hundred employees serve food to Inn guests each year. (During the past ten years, wait staff has set down over three million plates of food in front of Inn guests!) More than fifty cooks, pantry staff, and

dishwashers hide behind the dining room's swinging doors, flipping pancakes and steaks, stocking shelves, and scrubbing pans each season.[28]

The kitchen, now a modern marvel of food service equipment, has undergone major changes over the years. In 1929 it was enlarged and remodeled and the pantry removed. Twenty years later propane gas stoves replaced antiquated wood stoves. A bakery supplied the Inn's fresh baked goods at least through 1963. Also at that time, the Lodge rather than the Inn housed the butcher shop, but by the late 1960s refrigerated meats were stored in the Inn's basement. The kitchen was entirely remodeled in 1982 at a cost of nearly $2 million.[29]

Curtis Oliver Greer was head baker at Old Faithful Inn in 1936 and 1937. He baked bread by day and played cards by night, but admitted he did not have a "poker face." Greer lost his summers' earnings to his wily co-bakers.[30]

Jacqueline and Bruce Calhoun met at Old Faithful in 1951. Jacqueline was an Old Faithful

> They cleverly reserve the historic tour's room under the auspicious name "Robert Reamer."

The Inn's dining room staff posed for this photo, a long ago moment frozen in black and white, on August 23, 1915. *(Photo courtesy Haynes Foundation Collection, Montana Historical Society, Helena, Montana)*

Lodge waitress and Bruce, then stationed in Salt Lake City with the army, was a "dude" on a three-day pass. The smell of fresh-baked cinnamon rolls wafted from the Inn's bakery, tantalizing them one predawn morning. After a romantic stroll through the geyser basin, the young people gratefully accepted baked goods and coffee that were offered them by the baker.[31]

(Photo ©Jeff Henry)

Group of Old Faithful Inn employees, probably shot no later than 1910, apparently somewhere behind the Inn. Bessie Ferguson, from whose collection this photo was taken, is the woman in the center wearing a white dress and a white hat. *(Photo courtesy Bessie Ferguson Collection, Harry Child II)*

Old Faithful Inn viewed from the southeast in winter, with the East Wing in the foreground and the upper reaches of the Old House at right. *(Photo ©Jeff Henry)*

CHAPTER FOURTEEN

Savage Merriment at the Inn

*"A 'savage' was a recruited school teacher, student or someone looking for a vacation out 'West'
who will work...June to September for one of the concessionaires for 'peanuts' and return home, refreshed,
exhilarated, happy but probably broke, maybe in love, and come back year after year
until responsibilities prevail and end the affair."*

—WARREN McGEE, RAILROAD EMPLOYEE AND HISTORIAN, 1996[1]

I N YELLOWSTONE'S EARLY PERIOD, stagecoach drivers were nicknamed "savages" because of their uncultivated nature. Later the term described all concession employees. "Dudes" were park guests, "bubble queens" did laundry, "pearl divers" washed dishes, "heavers" were waitresses, "pack rats" were porters, and "pillow punchers" changed beds, to use a few "park speak" terms.[2]

One of the most sought-after jobs with park hotels was (and still is) "bellhop." In 1932, Inn bellman Henry Miller's birthday card read: "For the leader of the pack from your fellow wolves." A sense of camaraderie ran high among bell staff. Inn bellman and savage during the 1960s, Pierre Martineau said,

We worked very hard, made money and had a terrific amount of fun.

For many, working at Old Faithful Inn was the highlight of their lives.

His sentiments have been echoed time and again by other bell staff.[3]

These college-age employees were exceptionally creative at entertaining themselves and guests with their talents. According to Martineau, bellmen working for tips in the 1960s learned that a suitcase full of ladies' garments was a clever money-making scheme. They simply dropped the suitcase several times a day, brassieres and panties would immodestly tumble out, earning bucks *and* laughs.[4]

Bellhop Shari Kepner hauling a cart piled high, as usual, with the baggage of arriving guests, by Pierre's Garden in front of the Inn during summer 2001. *(Photo ©Jeff Henry)*

Bell captain Al Chambard remembered tremendous "esprit de corps" in the 1970s and compared the group's drive to a "sports team's athletic pursuit." Bellmen took great pride in the punctual arrival of tour bus guest's bags to their doors, never mind that there were no elevators. (The West Wing elevator was installed in 1988.) According to bellman Gary Gebert, there was a wager between bus tour drivers and bellmen in the early 70s. Who could get to the guests' door first: luggage-laden bellmen or guests? The loser supplied the evening's libations.[5]

Jamie Elsbury was the first female bellman at Old Faithful Inn. She took on the male-dominated position toward season-end in 1975, with the support of Chambard. "Bellman" was the job title regardless of gender in earlier days. Today the official title is "bell porter," but "bellhop" is more widely used. It is common today for women to serve as Inn bellhops.[6]

Bellman Roxanne Bierman said Inn bell staff bragged that "only tough, true, bellmen were at the Inn," because other park hotels had the luxury of elevators. She remembered strategically piling up a pyramid of at least 30 suitcases on the large, flat luggage carts, requiring one bellman to pull and two bellmen to push the cart up the ramp. Bierman said, "I carried at least four bags at one time; *I would not* be seen with a lesser load."[7]

"Christmas comes twice a year, once at home and once up here!" was a catchy sing-song phrase that Yellowstone savages used year after year. As the legend goes, there was a snowstorm one July in the park; roads closed and visitors were stranded. Employees decided to take advantage of the unusual weather and launched "Christmas" festivities.[8]

Where or when this custom began is unknown, but concession employees have renewed the park-wide celebration each year. At some point, savages moved "Christmas" to August 25th, paralleling the true holiday and its end of the year "feel." According to Homer Rudolf, the "holiday" was celebrated in a variety of ways and was dependent on the tenor of management, but "employees celebrated among themselves regardless."[9]

Savages decorated the little tree growing from a rock in the middle of the Firehole River from the 1970s through 2003. In the early 1970s, Miriam Johnston recalled that "Rangers would take the decorations off...and the next night the savages would put them back." Cathy Dorn remembered wading out to the little tree with other savages and decorating it with electric lights—powered by a car battery.[10]

Mary Fenner recalled that a medium-sized conifer tree was harvested by savages on "Christmas Eve" in the 1960s. Employees set up the tree in the Inn near the fireplace and decorated it with garlands of homemade popcorn and cranberries, and walnuts covered in foil or dipped in gilt paint. A spending limit of two dollars was imposed on packages piled beneath the spreading limbs of the tree. On "Christmas Day" names were put in a hat and the gifts were exchanged. The tree sparkled with the reflection of the Inn's candlestick lights and the lobby glowed with cheer as employees gathered round with mugs of cider and sang carols around the organ or piano. Beginning in 1984, Jim Cole led the festive song for nearly twenty years. Guests were welcome to join the festivities.[11]

Many of these "savages" returned year after year, forming a life-long camaraderie that even today they renew through regular employee reunions.

Christmas in Yellowstone is still celebrated today. Since 1998, Inn porter Carlos Smith has directed housekeeping staff to save burned-out light bulbs for children to paint and transform into colorful "Christmas" tree ornaments. Project tables were set up in front of the lobby fireplace and hot cider and cookies were offered enthusiastic artists young *and* old. Since 2000, the children's artwork has graced an artificial tree. Keeping with tradition, an employee-dressed Santa has made his lobby entrance from the Crow's Nest. Santa rode the big red fire engine through the Old Faithful area as part of the festivities in 2001-2003.[12]

In the 1950s, employees entertained guests at Old Faithful Inn and called their acts "savage shows." These evening performances featured employee talent and took the form of colorful song and dance, and clever skits. Similarly, in the 1960s, the Inn lobby hosted "talent shows"—in 1967 acts varied among a Tahitian dance, a Beethoven piano sonata, poetry, and a guitar duo. Inn guests crowded onto and filled all three levels of the lobby.[13]

The Inn's microphone was very accessible for a time and was a source of employee entertainment. One 1960s summer, a prankish bellhop occasionally proclaimed over the hotel's loudspeakers "midnight buffalo ride to Bunsen Peak," or "sale of geyser water in the gift shop" just before midnight or the gift shop's closing time.

In the early 1970s, a bus driver announced over the microphone: "Sam Sonite, Sam Sonite, your luggage is here." In 1971, bellhop Gary Gebert broadcasted that Plume Geyser was going off. "Ladies and gentlemen, this geyser erupts only every 27 years." The company lost 30-40 dinners as people fled unfed beyond the Inn's doors. For a time, Gebert cleaned bathrooms. Managers removed the mike from the bell desk. Today, the speaker system is used only for "legitimate" announcements, including the Inn's historical tours that occur each day.[14]

In the 1970s, "Frontier Days" was a creative manifestation of having fun while working at Old Faithful Inn. For three or four days, the Inn's front desk was made to look like an old-fashioned bank or post-office window, the bell desk became the local jail, and savages dressed in Old West attire: men donned western shirts, bolo ties, jeans, cowboy boots and hats, women dressed in blouses and homemade flouncy skirts, while other personnel wore Indian costumes. In the lobby, at least one year, girls danced their version of the can-can for hotel guests; other years there was a square dance. The men had a shoot-out and hung suspicious characters in the jail—all farcical events of course.[15]

Some savage activities were intended *only* for employees' own amusement and were often of dubious judgment. In the wee hours of morning, hot-potting or bathing in waters warmed from thermal features (*always* a dangerous nighttime pursuit even if in legal waters), scaling the lobby fireplace (yikes!), rappelling from the Crow's Nest (double yikes!), or riding the laundry chute from the top of the West Wing to the luggage room at the bottom of the West Wing, were among favorite employee amusements.[16]

An Inn chambermaid in the late 1920s, Anna Borgh recalled afternoon hikes with friends in the backcountry:

> *When we got to the chosen geyser he would fix the coffee pot and sit it into the edge of the geyser to be brewed—then we*

A Christmas card created for Christmas in August by lifelong Yellowstone area resident Bill Chapman.
(Courtesy Bill Chapman)

Christmas comes but twice a year, Once at home and once up here—

August 25, 1966

*would go on another short hike—by the time
we got back the coffee would be cooked.
However, one time when we got back the
geyser had erupted!*[17]

One night, a bellman imbibed too much liquor
and fell asleep. His cohorts "took his bed, sheet,
lamp, end table, and him, and placed them all in
the Crow's Nest in the top of the Inn." Needless,
to say, he was "unnerved" when he awoke.[18]

From at least the mid-1950s through the early
1970s, park locations held yearly "Beauty Pageant"
competitions. In the Old Faithful area, savages
of Old Faithful Inn, Old Faithful Lodge and
Campers' Cabins participated. Sponsored by Inn
bellmen in 1969, Jeane Blackburn participated in
swim suit, talent, and evening gown competitions
during the "Miss Old Faithful" competition
held at the Lodge. Her "talent" was "a patriotic
reading while playing patriotic medleys on the
piano"—timely entertainment that pleased the
Viet Nam War-era crowd. After winning
the title, Blackburn advanced to the "Miss
Yellowstone National Park" competition held
at park headquarters where she
was crowned "Runner-Up."[19]

Recycling *pays*. In the 1970s, Inn
bell staff gathered pop cans abandoned by geyser-seeking guests
with an end-of-the-season goal.
After a season of "cashing in"
the cans for the nickel deposits
that visitors had previously paid at
Hamilton Stores and Yellowstone
Park Company establishments,
the bell staff's coffers were plump
with thousands of dollars. A
"Bellmen's Banquet" was thrown
at year-end. According to bellman Gary Gebert (1969-1980),
the tradition "was going on long
before I got there." An entire
hotel floor might be rented in a
nearby town, or one year, a huge
cabin cruiser ferried partiers to
backcountry campsites along
Yellowstone Lake. Persuasive
bellmen wrote enticing letters
and invited the President of the
United States, governors from
surrounding states, and company
management. In the 1970s,

the last two always attended and President Nixon
considered it![20]

Today, bellhops throw a "toned-down" party
at Old Faithful—usually in August. Bellhops
and friends from around the park are invited to
partake in food and a long-standing bellhop
staple, "Yucca Flats," an icy citrus and maraschino
cherry fruit drink. Vodka is optional.[21]

Brian Raines described his feelings after leaving
the park his first year:

*Now that was a low time and somehow deep
in your heart you vowed to return. You knew
the truth…you were hooked.*

Many of these "savages" returned year after year,
forming a life-long camaraderie that even today
they renew through regular employee reunions.
The savages who serve guests in Old Faithful Inn
today will no doubt treasure their own stories in
years to come as their predecessors have and will
add to the storytelling success of the Inn.[22]

Hotpotting, or bathing and swimming in Yellowstone's geothermal waters, has long been a popular pastime for park employees. Michelle Roller is in the foreground of this scene at the Boiling River, a legal swimming hole where hot water originating from the Mammoth Hot Spring Terraces flows into the cool waters of the Gardner River, and the resulting mix renders a favorable temperature for bathers regardless of the season of the year. *(Photo ©Jeff Henry)*

Bellhop Kristen Arsenault on the widow's walk on the very top of Old Faithful Inn. One of the privileges of working as a bellhop at the Inn is putting up and taking down the flags on the top of the building. Here Kristen has taken down and folded one flag while a breath of evening air gently rolls Old Glory behind Kristen's left shoulder. *(Photo ©Jeff Henry)*

A beautiful interpretation of Old Faithful Inn
in winter by artist Lynn Bickerton Chan
of Yellowstone National Park.
(Painting courtesy Lynn Bickerton Chan)

CHAPTER FIFTEEN

Winter at Wonderland's Inn

*"The Inn...when covered with snow...its many angles and gables were decorated
by an artist who used white luster and diamonds, and who changed his design at the will of the winds."*

—BEULAH BROWN, EMPLOYEE AND TUTOR, 1924[1]

T HE INN GOES TO SLEEP IN FALL and hunkers down in repose while snows accumulate and winter winds whip up graceful drifts. Since its first full winter in 1905, winterkeepers have kept vigil over this queen of park lodges in keeping with one of Yellowstone's oldest traditions.

An assistant manager during the Inn's first decade, Mr. Morrisey, lived at the Inn during winter with his wife and young son Tom. Telephones were not reliable then during winter because of storms, so news, gossip, and mail delivered by cavalry patrol on skis or horseback were highlights twice a month. Tom recalled spending Christmas 1913 in the Inn as a teenager. He and his mother decorated the Inn with pine boughs and holly and bedecked the halls with festive ribbon. His father cut a huge tree—not to be swallowed by the lobby's

enormity—and placed a German-made nativity scene atop the Inn's front desk. Tom remembered few chores except stoking the great fireplace constantly and fixing the shutters to keep out the arctic cold. He did not mention his father shoveling snow, so perhaps Harry Child hired another man as winterkeeper.[2]

A winterkeeper's job was to keep the hotel roof free of heavy damaging snow, but he also safeguarded the building against theft and vandalism. Superintendent Horace M. Albright wrote in 1927: "There is a very heavy snow load at Old Faithful [Inn] and it keeps one man shoveling snow all winter to protect the roof." After every big storm, winterkeepers strapped crampons to their boots for better grip, climbed up to the Inn's roof, and used saw and shovel to clear the roof's numerous valleys that trap tremendous amounts of snow. They also shoveled smaller buildings in the area. Their job was difficult and dangerous physical work—consider the pitch of the Inn's roof![3]

Today, some winterkeeping is done on the Inn, but only what is deemed necessary—a fraction of what was done traditionally. Maintenance crews brace areas that are routinely assaulted by heavy snow loads.[4]

Winterkeepers rarely have misfortunes, but winterkeeper Howard O'Connor slid off the Old Faithful Inn roof in April 1912 and broke his leg. Even though U.S. Army soldiers unaccustomed to doctoring were able to set his leg with instructions from Fort Yellowstone's post surgeon, an ambulance was sent to fetch the unfortunate winterkeeper in mid-May. To clear the road, men laboriously hand-shoveled

In a continuation of the long tradition of winterkeeping in Yellowstone, Andy Ednisten on the left and Hill Theos pull a wire under the snow cornice on the mansard of the East Wing. Wiring the roof this way will precipitate a considerable avalanche and relieve the roof of a great deal of weight.
(Photo ©Jeff Henry)

snow drifts along the fifty-one mile route to Old Faithful.[5]

Tragedy visited Old Faithful during an April fifteen years later. A winterkeeper named Bauer picked some green plants growing in a thermal runoff channel and asked Park Ranger Charles Phillips to identify them. He mistakenly identified the plants as a species of wild parsnip. Anxious for some fresh greens, Phillips and Mr. and Mrs. Bauer partook in the wild plants. The Bauers became violently ill but recovered twenty-four hours later. Ranger Phillips was not so fortunate. The Bauers discovered Phillips dead on the ranger station kitchen floor. In reality, the plant was the deadly poisonous water hemlock that still grows along Myriad Creek behind the Inn.[6]

Why Phillips risked eating wild greens is especially curious, given the nearby greenhouse. Perhaps it wasn't utilized that winter. The Yellowstone Park Association built a 25' x 50' hothouse seven years prior to the Inn's emergence—its heat source came from nearly boiling geyser runoff. Lettuce, cucumbers and mushrooms were successfully grown using thermal waters, horse manure, and nearby silica formation. The greenhouse produced vegetables for patrons of Old Faithful Inn and the Upper Geyser Basin's earlier hostels. It was located south of the present lower gas station.[7]

One heavy block at a time, Wayne Tilley uses a two-handed scoop shovel to remove hard packed snow from the roof of the Bear Pit Lounge in the winter of 1983-1984. Wayne worked in Yellowstone in the 1970s, 80s and 90s.
(Photo ©Jeff Henry)

Mention of a newly conceived greenhouse came to light in 1913, so perhaps this later greenhouse was Old Faithful's second hot house. An Old Faithful Inn winterkeeper salvaged discarded windows from the "old" Canyon Hotel in 1913 and cleverly erected a wood-framed greenhouse over a hot spring pool near the hotel. Atop the thermal and barren ground, he built wooden boxes and filled them with imported soil for his vegetables. A newspaper write-up claimed the following: "Things grew in the hot house like wild fire, while the outside temperature ranged anywhere from 20-50 below zero." The heat was so intense, that keeping it cool enough was a serious challenge. Harry Child wrote: "we are going to try to raise fresh mushrooms so that Mrs. Underwood [the Inn's manager] can hand out some pretty good meals this summer." Tom Hallin remembered that the greenhouse was operational through the mid-1940s.[8]

Mr. and Mrs. Musser, year-round residents of the park, had three sons who grew up in the park, learning to ski as they learned to walk. In 1923, after spending six winters as winterkeepers for Old Faithful Inn, the Mussers asked Beulah Brown, a summer employee, to tutor their children for the winter. Mr. Musser utilized the geyser basin's hot water, ingeniously piping it into their house, root cellar, chicken house and greenhouse for the heat it provided. The warmth of the underground pipes made convenient snowless paths for easy walking. As a result, Beulah skied *and* hiked the geyser basins. Nature's subterranean plumbing produced warm, bare ground adjacent to four foot high heaps of snow! (This phenomenon continues today.)[9]

Winterkeeper Cliff Hartman shoveled snow at Old Faithful in the mid-1950s. He recalled that his winter abode was also heated by pipes zigzagging up the walls. He was one of three winterkeepers employed by the Yellowstone Park Company to lighten winter's toll on the Inn, Lodge and cabins, and other area buildings. Cliff remembered shoveling from sun up to sun down seven days a week.[10]

The winterkeeper's house still stands behind the Inn today—a testimony to those who chose this quiet life of isolation and hard work. In the early years of the park, there were no winter visitors, only year-round residents: bison, elk, ravens, and coyotes.

> "Things grew in the hot house like wild fire, while the outside temperature ranged anywhere from 20-50 below zero."

The Old Faithful green-house was located in the Myriad Spring thermal area behind Old Faithful Inn. It was heated by geothermal water piped in from the thermal area, and was used to grow greens for use in the Inn dining room in summer. Interestingly, it was also used by Old Faithful winterkeepers, those hardy souls who looked after the area's buildings in the off season, to grow fresh produce throughout Yellowstone's long, cold winters. The green-house was removed in the mid to late 1940s. *(Photo courtesy National Park Service, Yellowstone National Park Photo Archives)*

The winterkeeper's
house still stands
behind the Inn today
—a testimony to
those who chose this
quiet life of isolation
and hard work.

Old Faithful Geyser
erupting on a very
cold winter morning,
with Old Faithful Inn
visible at the lower left
corner of the frame.
(Photo ©Jeff Henry)

Old Faithful Inn at sunrise, with bellman Blue Bunch
a tiny figure putting up flags on the roof.
(Photo ©Jeff Henry)

CHAPTER SIXTEEN

Old Faithful Inn Admirers

From Presidents to Employees

"I was a "90 day wonder" with the Park Service in 1936...
As President, I visited Old Faithful for a speech on my dedication to the National Parks. I stopped at the Inn.
It hadn't changed much between 1936 & 1976: still very charming with the geysers almost next door."

—PRESIDENT GERALD R. FORD, 2003[1]

EVEN BEFORE OLD FAITHFUL INN WAS A CONVENIENT REFUGE in the Upper Geyser Basin, its location served as a presidential camp spot. President Chester Arthur camped beneath a tree near the present East Wing addition in 1883, twenty-one years before the Inn was built.[2]

Later Presidents followed his lead. President Warren G. Harding visited Old Faithful in 1923 and offered to autograph menus for young waitresses at the Inn's dining room. First Lady Florence Harding and her husband, keeping with the day's tradition, fed a bear cub named Max at the Continental Divide east of Old Faithful. President Calvin Coolidge visited Old Faithful Inn four years later. While her husband fished, First Lady Grace Coolidge strolled with Inn workers to a "show by the river that employees put on." President Franklin Delano Roosevelt and First Lady Eleanor Roosevelt visited Yellowstone National Park in 1937 and lunched at Old Faithful Inn.[3]

It is safe to say, since the Inn's genesis, several million folks have slept at the historic hotel.

Union Pacific Railroad postcard from the Panama-Pacific Exposition in 1915 showing some essential elements of the park to prospective visitors. Most prominent, of course, despite its recessed position in the composition, is the Old Faithful Inn.

Many other presidents and first ladies added to the Old Faithful Inn's history. President Ronald Reagan (Governor of California at the time) stayed at the Inn in the 1970s. To help celebrate the Yellowstone Centennial in 1972, First Lady Pat Nixon visited Old Faithful and stayed at the Inn. Old Faithful Geyser conveniently erupted during President Gerald Ford's address at Old Faithful during his presidential campaign in 1976. Lady Bird Johnson was a guest at the Inn in 1977. The next year, President Jimmy Carter visited Old Faithful Inn. In June 1989, President George Bush inspected a burned forest near Fountain Flats north of Old Faithful. President Bill Clinton and First Lady Hillary Rodham Clinton watched Old Faithful geyser erupt from the Inn's veranda in August 1995. First Lady Laura Bush stayed at the Upper Geyser Basin's famous hotel in 2002.[4]

During his thirty-five year bus-driving career (1947-1996) in Yellowstone, Joe "Popeye" Mitchell transported many distinguished guests to the Inn's doors. He remembered that the Prime Minister of Afghanistan and his staff, and in another year, the King of Nepal and his entourage, made the Old Faithful Inn their destination.[5]

Still other famous people have been guests at the historic hotel. A Hollywood "B" movie, *Yellowstone,* featured Old Faithful Inn and Yellowstone National Park in 1936, starring Andy Devine. A 1961 Disney movie, *The Yellowstone Cubs,* follows two black bear cubs into the Inn's kitchen where they wreak havoc and are reunited with their mother. Singers Roy Rogers and Dale Evans, entertainer Tennessee Ernie Ford, evangelist Billy Graham, and actors Henry Fonda and Vincent Price have rested at the Inn. The Three Stooges autographed pictures for front desk clerks in the late 1960s. More recently, actress Ali McGraw and actors Steve McQueen, Harrison Ford, Michael J. Fox and Jason Alexander have slept at the Inn. Musician John Denver also stayed at the historic hostel.[6]

An impressive Old Faithful Inn replica—amazingly built full-scale—was the center of attention at the 1915 Panama-Pacific Exposition in San Francisco, California. The Union Pacific Railroad, to promote railway travel to Yellowstone National Park via the West Entrance, hired "Smiling Joe" Kathrens to build the $500,000 Yellowstone National Park exhibit. Surrounded by expo-created mountain scenery and hiking trails, and fronted by a 50,000 square feet relief map of the park, the "Inn" was good advertisement for Yellowstone, and of course, for railroad business. The "Old Faithful Inn," described by a fair-goer as "a poem in rusticity," quickly became a social hub of the fair, entertaining guests with a symphony orchestra and an hourly spouting of "Old Faithful Geyser," engineered by Jack E. Haynes. The "Inn" model unfortunately stood only for the duration of the fair.[7]

Like the Old Faithful Inn replica of 1915, Florida's Disney World today offers up its Wilderness Lodge—modeled after Old Faithful Inn and other

National Park lodges of the west. It boasts an eight-story-high stone fireplace and a geyser that erupts "every hour on the hour from 7:00 a.m. to 10:00 p.m." Yellowstone's Old Faithful Inn and Geyser have had far-reaching effects and admirers indeed.[8]

Gingerbread, "Royal" icing, patience and engineering, landed the Summerfield family of Bozeman, Montana first prize for their awesome scale-rendition of Old Faithful Inn. Five adults labored five days over their entirely edible three foot by four foot creation. Their 2002 ginger-bread competition entry appropriately included the Inn's namesake geyser in eruption, board-walks, visitors and animals.[9]

Over the years, many Old Faithful Inn guests have returned repeatedly, renewing their "love affair" with the hotel. Since 1972, Glenn and Wanda Roberts and family of Lewistown, Montana have been guests at the Inn during its final weekend in the fall. In thirty-two years, the Roberts have relinquished their ritual only three times! (And yes, they have a favorite room!)[10]

More than one million guests have called the Inn their temporary home in the past decade alone. (Of course, this figure included guests who lingered beyond one night.) It is safe to say, since the Inn's genesis, several million guests have slept at the historic hotel. Hotel records claimed more than 650 overnight guests per day in recent years.[11]

Several years ago, the National Park Service estimated that more than 25,000 visitors experience an eruption of Old Faithful Geyser on a typical peak summer day. Most stop by Old Faithful Inn—as nearly an important icon to many as the geyser itself. During the day, we invite you to stop by the Inn's lobby after its namesake geyser has played. A great throng of passers-through can be guaranteed. Over the course of a year, approximately 2.6 million visitors pay homage to the Old Faithful area, with its geyser and historic hostelry.[12]

Perhaps Inn employees, through their daily intimacy with the hotel, hold it dear in a way that others cannot. Head baker in the mid-1930s, Curtis Greer loved the park and the Inn. In 1964, one of his dying wishes was for his son, Robert, to visit Yellowstone and Old Faithful Inn. Greer made his son "promise"—a pledge Robert finally kept in year 2000.[13]

Love of Old Faithful Inn is clearly all-consuming for some employees. Inn Executive Housekeeper in the early 1990s, Beth Casey named her daughter "Faith Abianne" and wrote "she clearly understands that she is named after the Inn and not the geyser!" Auditor in the early 1960s, Jo Ann Zimmerer Hillard expressed her sentiments for the Inn: "I don't know another thing in the park that can take its place. And that includes Old Faithful Geyser itself." Joe Swift and Lorraine Steiner (both former bellhops) exchanged vows December 14, 1996 at Old Faithful Inn. Like a sea captain sometimes officiates at weddings, the couple's bell captain, Charlotte Boscamp, married the Swifts on the Inn's widow's walk—on a chilly sub-zero pre-dawn morning.[14]

Throngs of visitors on the boardwalk around Old Faithful Geyser, with Old Faithful Inn in background. In 1904, the Inn's first year of operation, less than 14,000 people visited Yellowstone National Park. Now, 100 years later, the Old Faithful area alone receives 25,000 or more visitors per day during the peak of the summer season.
(Photo ©Jeff Henry)

Snowcoach drivers John Salvato, Melissa Stringham and Ken Keenan (left to right), with their snowcoaches parked in front of the Inn. It is rare nowadays for snowcoaches to park in front of the Inn, but these drivers were honored to carry the Olympic torch and its entourage to the front of the great building on January 27, 2002.
(Photo ©Jeff Henry)

CHAPTER SEVENTEEN

Bruins Around the Basin

Bear Stories from Old Faithful Inn

*"...the searchlight man chase[d] the bears with the powerful beam of light.
The bears are afraid of the electric glare, and ran like scared sheep whenever the rays were turned on them."*

—A. M. CLELAND, NPRR PASSENGER AGENT, 1904[1]

One of Yellowstone's famous grizzly bears, pictured here in the tawny vegetation of autumn.
Photo ©Jeff Henry)

OLD FAITHFUL GEYSER AND ITS NAMESAKE INN are not Yellowstone's only icons—the "bear" may be the most famous symbol of the world's first national park. In early park days, bruins soon learned that people meant food, but bears were well-loved despite their opportunistic and sometimes destructive behavior. In September 1903, a bear broke into Robert Reamer's residence, a store house and Army station kitchen in the Upper Geyser Basin, only to be shot the next day when it boldly charged an Army Private that was trying to shoo him away.[2]

Occasionally, bears could be viewed from the highest heights of Old Faithful Inn. An early postcard proclaimed: "Almost any evening or morning one may see from one to twenty bears eating in the vicinity of the hotel." Public bear feeding grounds were a source of lively evening entertainment for hotel guests around the park, and Old Faithful Inn was no exception. Black and grizzly bears impressed curious crowds who were often gathered behind flimsy fences that provided a sense of false security.

"Almost any evening or morning one may see from one to twenty bears eating in the vicinity of the hotel."

Clifford Allen described the scene in 1904:

Toward evening most of the party had returned and were wending their way in groups down to 'see the bears feed.' The road leads through a grove of pines in the rear of the hotel, in which are located the stables for the teams and also another camp of Uncle Sam's boys in khaki. The garbage dump is about a quarter of a mile back, and here the bears call for their supplies. The crowd that gathered there was sufficient to scare any kind of animal. Yet the bears made their appearance and rooted away for dinner entirely unconcerned. At first but one or two appeared, as big and fat as any corn-fed hogs, but later the whole drove, with several cubs, came out and secured their evening meal. Some counted nine, some eleven and some thirteen or more. The varying numbers were probably due to poor eyesight, caused by gazing on the backwoods tables in Larry's rathskeller [bar] in the basement of the Inn.[3]

In 1910, a little girl of five years offered a sugar cube in her small outstretched hand to a grizzly bear at the dump behind the Inn. An overeager photographer chose her because of her diminutive size. He was rather upset when out of fear she threw the sweet gift at the great bruin's gaping mouth, rushed back to her mother's skirts, and spoiled his photo opportunity. After learning that all bears are wild, even in a national park, the little girl confessed: "I made up my mind never again to offer food to any wild animal—not anywhere, not ever."[4]

Bears, following their hibernation instincts in fall, occasionally made use of the Inn's nether regions. In 1925, a female and large cub burrowed under Old Faithful Inn's foundation via a small trap-door for electrical cables. The bears clambered through the tiny tunnel of wires into the lobby. They wrecked havoc with leather seats, a window they interpreted as a "shortcut" to their den, and a barrel of salt, leaving salty-footprint evidence that they too, seemingly liked to explore the Inn's every nook and cranny.[5]

Winterkeepers discovered a sow and two cubs beneath the Inn's kitchen in February 1931, an auspicious hibernation residence that resulted in a bad turn for the bruin family. With the help of a wire hook and a hole cut into the floor, two rangers scooped up one of the tiny cubs. The drowsy sow bear made no objections regarding the change in her family size. The closed-eye three-pound baby was put in a parka pocket and accompanied the rangers on their one hundred mile ski trip to Mammoth. The cub "slept and howled alternately." They built fires along the trail to warm canned milk and fed the baby with an eyedropper—a poor substitute for its warm

8821 BEAR AT UPPER GEYSER BASIN, YELLOWSTONE PARK

Black bears eating garbage, some of which almost certainly came from the Old Faithful Inn. Watching bears feed in dumps was a popular pastime in the park's early days. Bleachers were set up at many dumps, from where tourists could watch as bears filed in from the forest as evening came on.

At least as late as 1937, black bears occasionally denned under Old Faithful Inn as winter approached.
(Photo ©Jeff Henry)

mother. "Barney," as they dubbed the young animal, quickly gained weight and was raised and studied by rangers at park headquarters.[6]

In 1932, ranger Frank Childs stopped one day at the barber shop behind Old Faithful Inn for a "shave and a haircut" that became *only* a haircut. After he noticed blood on the floor and the hotel nurse bandaging the barber's finger, Childs asked the barber about his injury. The barber said, "I was stropping my razor and watching some of the kitchen help feed that bear out there. Well, one of them almost got bitten. I got so excited that I let my razor slip and I cut the end of my thumb off." With the barber bandaged and ready to resume work, Childs tried to get comfortable in the hair-trimming chair. But the barber continued to eye the beggar bear, nervously fingering his razor. Childs told the barber, "I never shave my neck," an untruth that perhaps saved it.[7]

In 1937, a night watchman had an experience that "bears" telling. One morning he walked around the corner of the cashier's cage in the Inn's lobby and a bear surprised him, prompting him to jump over the top of the cage with remarkable ease. After he put in a call to a ranger, the bruin climbed up, up, up into the lobby's wooded atmosphere. When ranger Leon Evans shot the bear down from its elaborate tree house, the fatal shot must have reverberated throughout the Inn. The night watchman, a stuntman in winter, could not repeat his earlier leaping feat— he needed encouragement from the bear.[8]

Bonnie McDougall Hammar, a maid at the Inn in 1942, recalled that a bear had "gotten into the Inn and was terrorizing guests in the hallways." Rangers once again shot the bear after chasing it up around the mezzanine "until it could go no further." After a recent trip to Yellowstone, she noted that "there were not too many changes, just more roads and people and less bears."[9]

Beyond hotel proximities, black bears—mothers and cubs—begged alongside roads from amused and often willing motorists. An alarming number of both black and grizzly bears were destroyed during those garbage feeding days. During that time, about fifty people were injured each year by bears. In the 1970s, the National Park Service undertook an aggressive education program against people feeding bears at any location and campaigned for visitors to experience bears in their natural setting to reduce bear-human conflicts. Since then, human injuries have decreased to almost none.[10]

In 1972, when Yellowstone bears still associated food with people, the Upper Geyser Basin was the site of a story with a tragic ending. Late one

Sadly, even in contemporary Yellowstone there are still bears that are killed by park managers after the animals make the fatal association between humans and food. Note the bumper sticker on the park service pickup truck in this photo. *(Photo ©Jeff Henry)*

Saturday night, Old Faithful Inn guests' repose was interrupted by a young man bursting into the hotel shouting "Bear! Bear! Has my friend!" After having drinks at the Inn earlier, two young men returned to their illegal camp tucked in the trees above Grand Geyser. A grizzly bear, attracted to food left carelessly about the camp was having dinner. The bear, following its instinct to protect its food, charged the men and dragged one of them away. Park rangers discovered his body around 5:00 am.[11]

Sometime over a
century ago a bear in
Yellowstone's woods left
its claw marks on this
post that now stands in
the lobby of the Inn.
(Photo ©Jeff Henry)

CHAPTER EIGHTEEN

Nature Challenges Old Faithful Inn

*"In the East Wing, with the aftershocks,
the floor moved up and down like a wave; there was water everywhere."*

—GAYLORD MILBRANDT, BELLMAN, 2002[1]

YELLOWSTONE NATIONAL PARK VISITORS arriving from the west today travel a highway that snakes along the northern edge of Hebgen Lake, a manmade lake created by damming the Madison River just beyond the park's northwest boundary. The narrow nine-mile Madison Canyon sports three campgrounds, dude ranches, and roadside pull-outs and is a popular stopover for visitors to the area; its beauty and trout fishing reputation are a drawing card for many.

Shortly before midnight on Monday August 17, 1959, while most campers and distant Inn guests slumbered, one of the most severe earthquakes ever recorded on this continent rattled the Yellowstone area. Its tremendous force measured 7.5 on the Richter scale. The quake epicenter was one to two miles inside Yellowstone National Park's northwest boundary; seismic waves radiated out from that point. People felt the earthquake's initial shock as far away as the Pacific coast and western North Dakota.

> The Inn withstood the earthquake "because its sinews are flexible timbers."

New fault lines were active that night and old ones resurfaced. The slumped earth pulled violently away from itself creating what are called scarps. Land on one side of the fault line towered above the other by as much as 20 feet, when moments before the ground had been level.

Old Faithful Inn was badly shaken but survived the powerful Hebgen Lake earthquake on August 17, 1959. (Photo ©Jeff Henry)

Quake Lake behind rubble of the landslide precipitated by the 1959 earthquake. The lake is located on the Madison River a few miles west of Yellowstone National Park. *(Photo ©Jeff Henry)*

Mountain boulders released by the shifting land plunged to the valley below accompanied by massive mud, earth, and rock slides. This earth-wrenching quake was of giant intensity and had gigantic repercussions.

As the earth twisted, 3000 feet of highway slid into Hebgen Lake. Nearly simultaneously, a mile of road and river was buried in the narrow Madison Canyon when eighty million tons of mountain gave way. Hurricane strength winds tossed people, cars, and trees into the air like toothpicks. Due to the force of the quake, the waters of Madison River reversed their natural course, rushing upstream in a cacophony of water, rock, trees, and earth, and completely overwhelmed one of the campgrounds, Rock Creek, thus creating Earthquake Lake. Water levels continued to rise as Hebgen Lake sloshed over its rim at least four times, like water in a glass carried by an unstable toddler.

In the end, twenty-eight people lost their lives that night. All but two of them died as a result of injuries sustained while camping at Rock Creek. Nineteen were presumed buried by the slide. The Army Corp of Engineers bulldozed a spillway across the slide, draining waters potentially dangerous to downstream towns if the natural dam gave way. The Madison River flowed north once again.

A quake of that magnitude had other immediate ramifications throughout the area. Geothermal features' plumbing systems are hot-wired to earthquake activity. New and old fissures opened wide and wider and supplied even more hot water to around 150 normally quiet hot springs. They erupted in response. After the quake, Lower Geyser Basin's Clepsydra Geyser erupted continually—unusual for this geyser. (Today, it continues to play in a nearly constant eruptive state.) Old Faithful Geyser responded with only a slight interval increase that eased back somewhat by 1960.

In the Old Faithful area that night, nervous beauty pageant finalists stood on the Lodge recreation hall stage. Just before "Miss Old Faithful" was to be crowned, "the legs of the girls on stage started shaking and then the stage started shaking." Initially, there was a stampede as audience and contestants forgot about the sought-after title and ran to the exits.[2]

The timbers of Old Faithful Inn creaked, groaned, and popped as the massive structure responded to the earth's tremors. Broken water pipes in the East Wing sent water running down the hall. The hotel was immediately evacuated and mayhem ensued. Guests on the first floor jumped out windows. A bellman remembered, "Standing in the Inn was like standing on a bowl full of jelly."[3]

Gaylord Milbrandt, bellman that evening, remembered that the relatively quiet lobby suddenly became full of milling guests in various states of attire. Hotel guests anxious to leave eagerly paid the going rate of twenty dollars for bellmen to run up the stairs and down the vacillating halls to hurriedly pack their belong-ings. Milbrandt said "it was dangerous work and I didn't know if I was going to come out alive."

Hazardous duty also beckoned bellmen to the bowels of the Inn where they shut off the sprinkler systems that caused havoc upstairs.[4]

A sunset shot of Clepsydra Geyser in the Fountain Paint Pot area. In only one of a great many consequences of the 1959 earthquake to Yellowstone's thermal features, Clepsydra presently erupts more or less constantly. *(Photo ©Jeff Henry)*

Visitors soon discovered that they were trapped in the park. Uprooted trees, earth, and rock slides blocked most area roads. Park phone lines were down, making communication with worried loved ones back home impossible. To curtail panic, a ranger announced over a patrol car loudspeaker that no one was to leave. Instead, guests were given the option of spending the night in their automobiles or going to Old Faithful Lodge. People choosing the latter were shuttled via Yellowstone Park Company buses. Bellman Pierre Martineau and his co-workers earned their money that night. They hauled a sea of mattresses to the Lodge recreation hall where jittery guests spent the night and a concert of concerns was undoubtedly voiced.[5]

Old Faithful Inn was justifiably closed the day after the earthquake, but surprisingly, a handful of folks were permitted to occupy rooms in the West Wing on Tuesday, without meal service. An exodus of 7000 visitors, terrified by nature's power, fled the park the next day. Many employees, frightened by subsequent aftershocks, left for home, driving east over passable roads away from the earth's heaving. The Inn reopened for two days, but then closed for the remainder of the season.[6]

Minutes before the quake was felt at Old Faithful, baggage porter Robert Mautino was busy—not at work, but at celebrating his birthday with co-workers in the Bear Pit lounge. After a busy and exhausting summer toting luggage, Mautino recalled thoughts of quitting. He raised his champagne glass in a toast with his buddies before their exit from the Inn: "to our glorious summer, may it end soon." A week later, he was unemployed with no reason to stay and no more luggage to tote. The *Monthly Report of the Superintendent* in September admitted: "Visitation to the park declined sharply after the earthquake."[7]

The building's original exterior brick chimney was enclosed by log cribbing to stylishly match the Inn's porch supports and further add to its rustic frontier-cabin signature. But with the 1959 earthquake, the exterior chimney collapsed and bricks tumbled into all but two of the eight chimney flues. In that brief moment of seismic shake-up, the lobby fireplace could no longer host fires in all the hearths that encircled its girth. Though stable today, the lobby fireplace shifted one and a half inches from plumb that August

Park ranger looking at pavement fractured by 1959 earthquake, in Grand Loop Road in the Lower Geyser Basin. *(Photo courtesy National Park Service, Yellowstone National Park Photo Archives)*

night. After the quake, crews removed the cribbing and replaced the brick chimney with a forty-foot-high steel stack supported by guy wires as a future preventative measure.[8]

Shortly after guest evacuation, earthquake damage took its greatest toll on the Inn's original and south dining rooms. The dining room chimney collapsed and flying bricks peppered the roof with forty holes. Inside, the dining room fireplace cracked to within four feet of its hearth. Two fireplace rocks crashed through the south dining room ceiling and created gaping four-foot holes. They pierced and broke sprinkler system pipes that caused serious water damage to the Inn and continued their journey through the floor. As a result, the south dining room's oak floor had to be replaced. The fireplace was dismantled down to the arch over the hearth, not to be rebuilt until a 1980s restoration project.

If the earthquake had rattled Old Faithful Inn earlier or later, many lives may have been lost. Less than three hours earlier, the dining room had been full of dinner guests. If the quake had hit just twenty-nine minutes later, bellmen and porters accustomed to eating sandwiches and soup in the dining room after their shift was over might have died or sustained serious injury. Luckily, the only known injury was a sprained ankle as a guest leaped out of bed after the first tremor.

The shifting earth also seemed to have disturbed some animals around the Inn. A number of black bears abandoned their forest retreat and hung around the bustling Inn after the quake. Katherine Miller Jensen remembered that she occasionally had to detour around the bruins during her night-long vigil of serving hot chocolate and coffee to Inn refugees beneath the Inn's porte cochere. The bears were docile and did not seem to be interested in food. Rather, Jensen felt they were somehow comforted by human companionship. Seldom glimpsed in the park, a number of snakes also deserted their beds and were seen slithering along the creek behind the Inn the morning after the earth's trembling.[10]

Following the 1959 earthquake, a myth has prevailed: because some of the Inn's upper staircases and deck supports had twisted in the quake, visitors were no longer allowed beyond the third floor balcony. Actually, the privilege to peer down from the heights of the Crow's Nest or the widow's walk had been taken away eleven years earlier, a manager's prerogative to safeguard his guests. After World War II, the number of people that visited the Inn greatly increased and the Inn's upper reaches could not support the number of people who visited the Inn.[11]

Amazingly, the towering Old Faithful Inn sustained relatively little damage from the quake, though repair work ensued for two months after the hotel closed its doors. Sixteen years before the quake, lobby roof purlins had been bolstered with diagonal timbers as a whopping ninety-three inches of snow pack was recorded at Old Faithful the previous winter. These "new" timbers were darker in color and were easy to locate in the upper limits of the lobby. (Restoration architects will probably remove these braces in 2005 which are pushing the Old House wings away from the lobby.) Heavy snow loads gave the Inn's fanciful props—both inside and outside—new purpose: crucial structural integrity. Perhaps the new purlins and the fortuitous added support of Reamer's decorations helped the Inn withstand the 1959 earthquake.[12]

Restoration architects discovered that the earthquake traveled diagonally through the Inn's lobby —from northwest to southeast. The wings helped stabilize the Old House. If the quake had rippled through the lobby south to north, Old Faithful Inn would probably have been lost. According to one park ranger naturalist, the Inn withstood the earthquake "because its sinews are flexible timbers."[13]

And so the blessed Old Faithful Inn survived. The earthquake of 1959 was a not-so-gentle reminder that we are but witnesses to the earth's powerful forces, forces that cannot be controlled by human will or design. Yellowstone National Park and her geothermal unrest remain today constant reminders of greater forces at play.

In spite of the travails of the Hebgen Lake earthquake, which caused an early end to the tourist season in 1959, Old Faithful Inn survived to enjoy the tranquility of the following winter. (Photo ©Jeff Henry)

CHAPTER NINETEEN

A Firestorm Over the Inn

A Personal Account of the 1988 North Fork Fire by Jeff Henry

"The darkness, the winds, the embers everywhere, and the incredible pandemonium of people and vehicles and fire hoses all combined to give me a horrifyingly surreal sensation."

—LEE H. WHITTLESEY, NATIONAL PARK SERVICE RANGER,

RECALLING SEPTEMBER 7, 1988, AT OLD FAITHFUL

T HE SUMMER OF 1988 marked the beginning of my twelfth year in Yellowstone. That summer I worked as a National Park Service Ranger stationed at Madison Junction, 16 miles north of Old Faithful. Though law enforcement certified, most of my time was spent working on resource management projects. When it became apparent in late July that Yellowstone was on the threshold of an exceptional fire season, the NPS assigned me to photograph the fires for the park archives. With the exception of one day off, I spent every day for the next two months engaged in that project in nearly all parts of the park.

Initially the Old Faithful area was threatened by the North Fork Fire shortly after a woodcutter in Idaho's

Sunset at Old Faithful on the sixth was filtered through two large fire columns to the west, and the area was bathed in an ominous orange light.

he afternoon of
eptember 7, 1988 at
Old Faithful Inn. In dense
moke and violent wind,
refighters Ken Hansen
eft) and Nick Ricardi
noot water onto the
outh side of the Old
House. Note the intensity
f the wind as indicated
y the American flag on
op of the building.
Photo ©Jeff Henry)

Targhee National Forest started the blaze with a carelessly discarded cigarette on July 27. Although the North Fork was attacked by smokejumpers and other firefighters on the first afternoon of its existence, the fire escaped their efforts and within a few days was throwing up tremendous columns of smoke capped by huge convection clouds as it burned across the Madison Plateau northwest of Old Faithful. For several days in late July and early August the smoke columns and clouds were readily visible from Old Faithful, and the fire was close enough to the complex that ash sifted down from overhead smoke onto the Old Faithful Inn and other buildings in the area. Fascinatingly, some of the ash particles were perfectly recognizable as conifer needles or twigs. Somehow the particles retained their integrity as they burned and were swept skyward in the conflagration, then were carried considerable distances by overhead winds. They would, however, disintegrate instantly when I touched them with the tip of my finger.

Massive fire line construction along the near flank of the North Fork kept it away from Old Faithful as Yellowstone's prevailing southwesterly winds swept the fire across the park toward the northeast. Ultimately the gigantic fire would achieve a perimeter encompassing 500,000 acres, but for about a month it seemed that Old Faithful had been left safely in the monster's wake. In late August and early September, however,

Yellowstone experienced a period of anomalous east and northeast winds which, in the military hyperbole so favored by firefighters, outflanked the fire lines constructed in August to shield the Old Faithful complex. Having outflanked the fire lines to the south, any reasonable person looking at a fire map could foresee that the North Fork would have an unobstructed run at Old Faithful when the normal southwesterly winds returned.

By the afternoon of September 5, and certainly by the afternoon of the sixth, it was obvious that such a run was well underway. Sunset at Old Faithful on the sixth was filtered through two large fire columns to the west, and the area was bathed in an ominous orange light. Smoke from the fire columns blew directly toward the Inn and other buildings in the development, and once again ash drifted down from the sky into the complex. A dry cold front with powerful winds was forecast for September 7, but Old Faithful and the rest of Yellowstone nonetheless remained open to visitors.

On the morning of September 7, I temporarily was diverted from the fire documentation project to help prepare for the fire's arrival at Old Faithful, even though some park officials publicly claimed there was only a one in three chance of that happening. I drove a large stake-bodied dump truck from Madison, met a crew at Old

Old Faithful Inn silhouetted against the sunset on the evening of September 6, 1988. The proximity of the North Fork Fire and its location upwind from Old Faithful made its arrival in the area only a matter of time.
(Photo ©Jeff Henry)

Firefighters with infrared spotting scopes, used to see focal points of heat through dense smoke, on the widow's walk of Old Faithful Inn in the early afternoon of September 7. A short while later the men abandoned this lookout and hastened down, but not before stating their certainty that the building and everything else in the area was doomed. *(Photo ©Jeff Henry)*

Faithful, and together we moved a large number of road and trail signs from the Park Service sign cache to an empty parking lot near the Old Faithful Ranger Station. An old log structure near the forest on the west edge of the Old Faithful complex, the sign cache was one of four such structures in its immediate neighborhood. Defending the four structures so close to the trees was considered difficult and a low priority, but the signs themselves represented a large investment of labor and were considered worth saving. When the fire struck later in the day, the sign cache, while unprotected and very close to intense fire in the nearby forest, inexplicably would survive. Capriciously, the fire would burn two of the other three nearby cabins. The signs we removed also survived, somehow not igniting when a whirlwind of sparks and embers blew through the parking lots near the Old Faithful Ranger Station and the Old Faithful Inn later in the day.

After moving the signs, my crew and I next loaded the stake truck with firewood that had been piled adjacent to some NPS houses in the residential area on the west side of the Grand Loop Road, opposite Old Faithful Inn. By the time we finished loading the wood, the fire's arrival at Old Faithful seemed imminent, so I parked the truck in front of the ranger station, grabbed my cameras and headed for the widow's walk on the roof of the Old Faithful Inn.

I found two firefighters on top of the Inn, each equipped with an infrared scope he could use to see through smoke to identify hot spots in a fire. They were using the scopes to scan the timbered ridges west of Old Faithful, beyond which the North Fork Fire had created a large bank of smoke. Slurry bombers were dropping their loads of red fire retardant on the near edge of the pall of smoke, and several helicopters were flying about as well. Some of the helicopters were carrying buckets from which they dumped water on the fire, while others were unencumbered and presumably carried observers to scout the fire.

Pretty quickly after I arrived on the roof of the Inn the fire to the west became more active and organized itself into a long front. The day had been breezy since dawn, but now the winds picked up to gale force.

From personal experience I can say that the winds were very, very strong, so strong that I distinctly remember thinking they would have made September 7, 1988 memorable even if there had been no fire.

The North Fork Fire arriving at the parking lot on the south side of Old Faithful Inn. The running crown fire illustrated here, as spectacular as it appears, was largely obscured by smoke when the photo was taken. *(Photo ©Jeff Henry)*

I've heard variously that the winds were 50 to 80 miles per hour that afternoon at Old Faithful. From personal experience I can say that the winds were very, very strong, so strong that I distinctly remember thinking they would have made September 7, 1988 memorable even if there had been no fire. Case in point: a tripod has a widely braced stance and offers little sail area to the wind, but on several occasions that afternoon on the roof of Old Faithful Inn I had to catch my tripod to keep it from blowing over.

As I went out the Inn's back door to the south parking lot, I thought I was leaving the building for the last time.

The North Fork Fire had several weeks of momentum, it had an abundance of fuel parched by extreme drought, and on September 7 it was driven to explosiveness by overpowering winds. Behind the smoke a blitzkrieg of fire and wind was bearing down on the Old Faithful area. How high were the flames? I can't say for sure. Most of the time the flames were hidden by smoke, but once in a while the smoke would part and I could see flames I reckoned to be three or four times the height of the trees, realizing that some lodgepole pines are around 100 feet tall. Usually the flame

presented itself as a wall, a long curtain of fire that advanced in an undulating, flickering line. But sometimes huge balls of flame would fly out from the front as the wind caught a pocket of gasified fuel and flung it forward as it ignited. Some of these fireballs appeared to be several hundred yards in diameter and were hurled several hundred yards ahead, where they would ignite new pockets of fire in advance of the front. As the fire advanced it seemed to intensify. Visually the effect became one of a gigantic rolling wave of flame as the fire sucked air in at ground level while the wind aloft, blowing in the opposite direction, blew the crest of flame forward. The flame really did roll forward and curl under itself at its base, like an ocean wave breaking in the surf. At other times I could see spinning spirals of fire, and couldn't help but think of flaming tornadoes. These visual impressions were caught in snatches, visible only when the vagaries of wind and fire opened the smoky curtain. But the tremendous roaring of the fire was always there, even when you couldn't see it.

On top of the Old Faithful Inn the two firefighters had put down their infrared scopes—the images in the scopes had long since become too bright for their eyes to bear. And by this time no special technology was needed to see what was coming toward the Old Faithful area. Also by this time all the other people who had gathered on the roof of the Inn had beat a hasty retreat downward; the spotters and I were the only ones left on the widow's walk. Talking among themselves and to me while they donned fire protective masks and gloves, the spotters agreed that at this point there was nothing that could be done to avoid the catastrophe that in their view was now inevitable. For my part I could see no reason to disagree. From where I was on top of the Inn it looked as though the buildings of the area were about to be incorporated into the firestorm and that a lot of people probably were going to die. The spotters and I left the widow's walk on top of the Inn and hurried down the half log stairs to the lobby floor. As I went out the Inn's back door to the south parking lot, I thought I was leaving the building for the last time.

In the parking lot I was struck by a blizzard of sparks and embers as a billow of smoke surged just overhead and light nearly vanished from the day. There were still many visitors in the area, and I had visions of taking one or two families by the hand and leading them to the geyser plains in front of the Inn, where I had further visions of squatting in the water of the Firehole River while we watched the Old Faithful Inn and other buildings burn. In the chaos that seemed certain to ensue I thought that would be the best I could do. Fire had already entered the Old Faithful complex—I could hear explosions behind the

Snow Lodge as cabins burned and heated air inside the structures expanded to the point where the cabins burst. The explosions made me think of artillery bombardment in a war zone.

Back at the Inn a large number of firefighters had gathered with hoses connected to fire hydrants. Others were on hand with water pumping trucks. These people were wetting down the sides of the building as high as their hoses would spray. The sprinkler system on the roof of the Inn also had been activated and water deluged over the eaves. All this was a welcome surprise, for just a short time earlier in the day protection for the Inn had seemed very spare. I saw all this activity as I gravitated back toward the Inn, waiting to see exactly what was going to happen before I made that last ditch move toward the geyser basin. Those brave firefighters, some of whom had even stationed themselves perilously on the flat roofs of the East and West wings of the Inn, deserve great credit for saving the historic structure. Without their efforts to keep the walls and roofs of the Inn wet, the building certainly would have ignited in the fiery holocaust that blew in that afternoon. Indeed, the very air seemed to be on fire. Several times that day I saw isolated bits of fuel, things like upturned stumps in the geyser basins or fallen logs on islands in the parking lot, burst into flame in seemingly spontaneous ignition, as though exhaled upon by some fire breathing dragon.

Unidentified firefighters positioned on the roof of the East Wing shooting water toward the Old House. All the figures in the photo are merely silhouettes because of the darkness brought on by the immense amount of smoke that was present. *(Photo ©Jeff Henry)*

In addition to the ground blizzard of sparks and embers that swirled around our ankles and calves, larger embers showered down upon the Inn like fiery ejecta from an erupting volcano. A little known fact is that one of the Inn's outbuildings actually did catch fire that day. The old laundry building, the building presently used as a recycling collection center, caught fire on its roof. Fortunately the spot fire was quickly put out by some alert concession employees who happened to be nearby.

As I moved around the Inn snapping pictures of firefighters at work, someone shouted above the infernal roar of the wind that there was fire on Observation Point, above Geyser Hill on the other side of the Firehole River from Old Faithful Inn. It was true—windborne fire had leapt completely across the Old Faithful area, including all the parking lots and bare geyser plains, and ignited new fire on the other side of the basin. The fire above Geyser Hill grew quickly, and soon ran over the hill and out of sight beyond Observation Point. Now Old Faithful Inn was literally surrounded by fire. Radio traffic on the Park Service handset I carried confirmed the obvious, that the road in both directions from Old Faithful was blocked by fire.

And so it went for some period of time; it's hard hard to say how long. Firefighters continued

hosing the Inn, a few small structures continued to blow up as they burned on the south flank of the Old Faithful development, and spot fires appeared in small plots of trees around the Inn and Old Faithful Geyser. Gradually, as the afternoon wound down and the main front of the fire moved off to the east, the immediacy of the situation lessened. Slowly it became safe to believe that the Old Faithful Inn and the other major buildings of the area were going to survive and that no one would be killed or seriously injured in the afternoon's conflagration. Some sources claim that a wind shift of a few degrees blew the main front of the North Fork Fire off course just before it hit the Old Faithful area, but I have never been able to find the source behind this assertion. I can't imagine anyone on scene that afternoon having the necessary equipment, or the presence of mind to use it had it been available, to make such an observation. My personal interpretation is that a long front of fire arrived at Old Faithful from the west, and that the segment of the line that would have intersected Old Faithful Inn and the main body of the complex lost much of its awesome momentum when it encountered areas of sparse fuel between itself and the development. The main park highway, the National Park Service housing area to the west of the road, and the Myriad Springs area were some of the elements that created the fire break that

Firefighter Amy Recker hosing the boiler house behind Old Faithful Inn. Much credit must be given to the firefighters who worked so valiantly that day, often at considerable peril to themselves. Without their efforts Old Faithful Inn almost without question would have been lost.
(Photos ©Jeff Henry)

contributed to the survival of the Inn. I think the expansive parking lots adjacent to the Inn were especially important fire breaks. Dichotomously, the line of fire that struck the south flank of the development burned through unbroken and heavy fuel right into the Snow Lodge cabin area, and that's where most buildings were lost. Fortunately, most of the buildings that burned were relatively inconsequential, several of them being employee cabins that had been slated for removal anyway.

As evening came on, a press conference was held on the steps of the Old Faithful Ranger Station (not the existing ranger station but a building that has since been removed). I conversed with some reporters present at the press conference, reviewing the incredible events we had witnessed earlier in the day. Some of the press people were veterans who had spent time in many global hot spots on dangerous assignments. It was impressive to me that at least two of these people told me that they had been more frightened that day as the fire was bearing down on Old Faithful than they had been earlier in their careers in places like Saigon and Beirut.

For my part I circulated around the Old Faithful area for several more hours, looking around to see what had been burned and feeling thankful for what had not. Several times I returned to the Inn, once even walking completely around its circumference. Some vigilant firefighters were still on duty, standing guard through the smoky night while remnants of fire snapped and crackled in the distance. When I finally decided to leave the area late that night, probably 1:00 or 2:00 in the morning after the road north to my summer home at Madison had cleared of fire to some degree, I sat in the cab of my big park service truck with its load of firewood and gave a last look at the Inn. The Old House loomed large in the smoky darkness, against a backdrop of glowing spots of fire over on Observation Point, and reminded me of William Vandivert's famous photograph of St. Paul's Cathedral standing defiant amidst the smoke and dust of the London Blitz of 1940. I'm sure Londoners couldn't have been more thankful that their cathedral had survived the Nazi bombing than I was that the Old Faithful Inn had survived the North Fork Fire. I also felt very grateful that I had had the privilege to be present at Old Faithful on such a historic day.

CHAPTER TWENTY

The Inn Restored

*"to do this kind of work it takes someone who is a little bit crazy,
a person willing to crawl anywhere on the building such as across the roof and into every nook and cranny
that might yield the data necessary to do a proper restoration."*

—ANDY BECK, RESTORATION ARCHITECT, 1993[1]

O NCE INSIDE ANY CAVERNOUS BUILDING, a state or national capitol building for example, a person's first notion—a reflex, really—is to try to visually absorb the enormity of the dome. The same is true with Old Faithful Inn. As of this writing, there is a worn spot in the floor of the lobby where people have paused and reacted—often slack-jawed with wonder—to the lobby of immense proportions offered up to their gaze. It has been compared to a "medieval cathedral,"[2] the "skeleton of some enormous mammal seen from within,"[3] or to an enormous tree house. People, generally talkative upon entering the Inn, often whisper out of respect for the sacred.

One view of the ornate woodwork seen when looking up from the lobby floor
(Photo ©Jeff Henry)

Main stairway on the second floor, east side of the lobby.
(Photo ©Jeff Henry)

People, generally talkative upon entering the Inn, often whisper out of respect for the sacred.

The Inn's cedar shingle roof was replaced in 1980-81. Three layers of old shingles had to be stripped off before new shingles could be placed. Plastic was laid over the roof in the interim to keep weather out of the building's interior, as illustrated in this photo shot in October of 1980. *(Photo ©Jeff Henry)*

Climb to the balconies above the lobby for further evidence of tribute, and note how the log stairs have been polished to a comfortable divot by generations of appreciative folks. Run your hand along the richly patinized gnarly wood banisters as countless hands have done before you.

Over the years, the Inn has been loved, appreciated, documented in journals and photo albums, and etched into memories. Ask your father, grandmother, neighbor, or friend if they have visited Old Faithful Inn. Do an internet search on Old Faithful Inn of Yellowstone National Park. You will be guaranteed a behemoth number of "hits," as an Inn of this pioneering style nestled in this unique place creates lasting impressions that people love to share.

Whenever anything is so cherished, it must be cared for. After many years of use coupled with structural alterations to accommodate guests' changing needs, major rehabilitation was needed by the 1970s for the Inn's ongoing health. The Old Faithful Inn Restoration Project began in 1979 with diligent research. Hard physical work followed for ten years. Identified concerns included structural and aesthetic integrity, outdated plumbing and electrical systems, a potential asbestos hazard, and other safety concerns as well as comfort. Top of the list however, was to keep as much of the "historic fabric" as possible.[4]

Because Old Faithful Inn is open during the summer season, most of the restorative work was done during the cold of many winters. Andy Beck, architect with the National Park Service's Denver Service Center, was project leader from 1980-1983. Beck wrote, "with snow falling at a rate of 3 feet a day, and temperatures of 37 degrees below zero, the crew never shut down one day due to weather the entire winter."[5]

Ninety percent of the 1980s restoration work involved shingle and log work. The foremost project was reroofing the Inn. Challenges included shoveling snow before work could begin, tearing off up to three layers of old shingles, and precisely replacing the western red cedar shingles. The siding shingles were not run-of-the-mill, but special 6" by 36" no taper ¼" redwood. The fancy old chevrons were photographed and their replacements were hand-carved by artisans, echoing efforts in the early twentieth century. Shinglers hand-nailed 1000 squares. Their hammer volleys punctuated the geyser basin, paying homage to the working carpenters who originally built the Inn.[6]

Logs that were deemed unsound were replaced, totaling hundreds of feet. After a thorough structural analysis, steel rods were inserted in log supports wherever tension members were. Sill logs were replaced (imagine jacking up an Inn section four stories high!).[7]

Permission to gather building materials within park boundaries was not available. For two weeks, crews searched nearby national forests for whimsical branch decorations. They held up contorted and twisted branches and hoped for a perfect match. They looked for the nod of approval just as workers must have done with their architect in 1903-1904.[8]

A serendipitous meeting between visitor and architect during the 1980s project resulted in the resurrection of a bit of history. Someone recalled twelve cartoon panels in the Bear Pit carved from wood from a 1941 trip to the park. He had kept a brochure about the comic artistry for forty years! After a gallant research effort, nine of the panels original to the Inn in 1936 were discovered in a Gardiner warehouse. Five were restored and returned to their original home in today's Pony Express Snack Shop.[9]

To further preserve this historical find, the decision was made to replicate the original wooden panels in glass with even more detail. Artisans hand-sculpted and sand-blasted eight glass partitions that spanned the columns separating lounge from restaurant and guaranteed a grin. Since 1988, these hilarious renditions of Yellowstone animals personified have entertained guests. For posterity, one of their makers subtly etched his initials in the panels.[10]

Other 1980s projects included a new kitchen, dining-room fireplace reconstruction, the replacement of historic glass with glass of the same vintage salvaged from a Helena synagogue, and ten new sisal lobby mats stenciled with original area rug patterns.[11]

At Old Faithful Inn, Reamer balanced beauty with functionality and comfort, keeping in mind the needs of the Inn's guests. When the nearly 7.4 million-dollar restoration project was completed in 1989, the Inn was back in shape, ready to greet its guests with updated comfort and convenience without sacrificing its sacred historical statement.[12]

After the restoration project, Old Faithful Inn was awarded all three possible Presidential Design Awards. Architects were lauded for their design and historic preservation efforts. The final award, the "President's Award for Design Excellence" was bestowed on restoration architects Andy Beck, Tom Busch and Paul Newman by President Bill Clinton in the White House in April 1994. Though Robert Reamer apparently never called attention to his architectural successes, he no doubt would have been proud.[13]

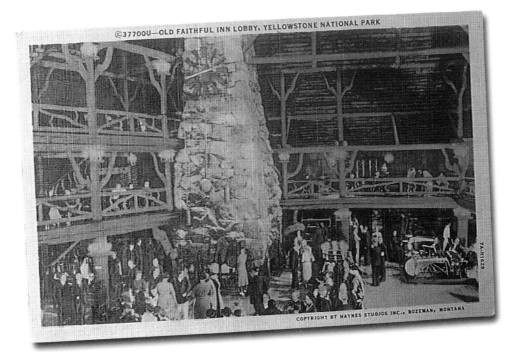

©37700U—OLD FAITHFUL INN LOBBY, YELLOWSTONE NATIONAL PARK

COPYRIGHT BY HAYNES STUDIOS INC., BOZEMAN, MONTANA

No. 135   LOBBY OLD FAITHFUL INN–YELLOWSTONE PARK.   HAYNES-PHOTO.

The area around the Inn's massive fireplace originally
featured a sunken floor and a handrail which parti-
tioned the area from the rest of the lobby. The sunken
floor and handrail will be reinstated during the renovation work planned to begin in the autumn of 2004.

The 2004-2006 Renovation Project

A Birthday Present for the Inn

"When we build, let us think that we build for ever."

—JOHN RUSKIN, SOCIAL THEORIST, 1819-1900[1]

THE NATIONAL PARK SERVICE DETERMINED IN 2001 that the Old House needed significant upgrading to meet today's standards of seismic safety. The 1959 earthquake separated Old House walls from its foundations and wing additions. To better serve Inn guests, walls were moved or removed through time, but Old House stability was sacrificed. The foundation beneath the great fireplace was structurally inadequate.

The restoration team perceived the project slated for 2004 as a "birthday present" for the Inn from the beginning. The upgrade will be launched in the fall during Old Faithful Inn's centennial year. The historic hotel will be pulled back together. Wings will be anchored to the Old House and foundations and new walls will provide critical support. Architect James McDonald projected the Inn's condition after the project completion: "The Inn will still move, but will act as one, instead of in pieces."[2]

McDonald believed the giant fireplace's four miniature corner hearths (only seven inches at the base) were "kindling" fireplaces. When the fireplace was built, the greater volume of air in the larger hearths would have quickly extinguished a small-stick fire, so personnel started fires in the tiny fireplaces first. Once ignited, the kindling fire was scooped out and moved to the larger hearths where the nursery fires were augmented by sizable lodgepole pine rounds.

Planners debated a possible propane conversion of the great fireplace, but decided that the Old Faithful Inn fireplace will continue to burn lodgepole pine as it has since its creation, a tribute to Reamer, his stone masons and a century of contented guests.

Because of the historic nature of the lobby fireplace, restoration architects will strengthen its base almost invisibly. During the off-season of 2004-2005, a new foundation will be poured beneath the giant hearth and encompass its existing rubble support system. Four concrete piers will consume the four "kindling" fireplaces. While it is unfortunate to lose these historic miniature fireplaces, the new piers will anchor the fireplace to its new foundation and substantially increase its seismic stability.

Chimney brick fell into two of the four large flues during the 1959 earthquake and after forty-five years, will be extricated from the top. All four large flues will then be scoured clean. Once clear, workers will line the flues with a reinforced concrete wall.

After restoration, bellhops like their predecessors, can tender a blaze in all four large hearths that encircle the grand fireplace. With the gift of restoration in fall 2004, guests will be able to once again appreciate the glow in Reamer's behemoth masonry heater at the east, west, north and south.

Reamer apparently envisioned the hearth experience as an intimate one. Early postcards clearly show a sunken and railed area around the fireplace. This cordoned area will be reinstated by the start of the 2005 season. What a privilege it

One of the "kindling" fireplaces on the corner of the massive hearth, with some of the large wrought iron tools built on a scale to match the hearth. In an effort to strengthen the structure, the kindling fireplaces will be walled up in the renovation scheduled to begin in the fall of 2004. *(Photo ©Jeff Henry)*

will be to be taken back to the Inn's opening days with the help of modern day architects and crews!

Carpenters will also replace the worn and weary lobby floor. Nails have popped up through the floor boards, their heads sanded and worn away through time by Inn guests and employees. The original pine floor was replaced with maple planks in 1940. Since the beginning, guests have paused and pondered the lobby dimensions just a few paces from the Inn's welcoming doors. Evidence of their gratitude, like a well-worn beloved backcountry trail, will be erased by fresh maple boards in the Inn's centennial year. Guests will tread for the first time upon the new floor-boards July 1, 2005.

Old House guest rooms will undergo only cosmetic changes during the project. Workers will resurrect more of the rooms' original charms, enhancing the guest experience. Old House east wing rooms will be renewed first and are slated for completion by the Inn's opening date in

For over a century Old Faithful Inn has endured, while generations of visitors and employees alike have come and gone. *(Photo ©Jeff Henry)*

carpet will be inserted in the center of the refinished fir floors.

By project end, two separate guest rooms that are accessible to persons with disabilities will be created from three guest rooms. The Old House "experience" of a "bath-down-the-hall" will be preserved for guests in these two rooms. Rooms with bath will also be accessible, as they were prior to the restoration. All floors of the Old House, the sunken fireplace area, the gift shop, and the updated and enlarged public restrooms will either be accessible via West Wing rotunda elevator or ramps. (The West Wing ramp and the bell porter's ramp was replaced in summer 2003 to meet accessibility standards.)

One housekeeping room and two administrative offices will return to their original purpose and serve as guest rooms. After the project concludes, the Inn will gain two guest rooms, bringing the hotel's room count to 329.

summer 2005. Guests will stay in renovated Old House west wing rooms a year later. Though internet service will be provided in the breezeway and rotunda connecting the East and West Wings to the Old House wings, Old House rooms will remain without phone jacks, echoing the early day guest experience. Insulation will be tucked wherever feasible into the previously uninsulated hotel to boost privacy. The noisy steam radiators of yesteryear will be replaced by new radiators more similar to the original style and the heating system will be upgraded to hot water heat.

Workmen will update electrical and fire suppression systems concurrently with the lobby and room projects. Much of these systems' infrastructure will lie buried in the floor, reducing visual impacts. Antiquated cloth electrical wires will be disconnected, but will continue to snake along logs in the lobby's upper reaches.

Guest room floors originally had small scatter rugs. To imitate guest rooms' early floor coverings, but also increase safety, a slightly raised

Frequent Inn guests will notice the return of two second floor mezzanine walls and the outward shift of the Pony Express's east wall into the lobby. Carpenters will erect these new walls by July 1, 2005. They will resume their original load-bearing positions and strengthen the hostel's defense against another strong earthquake.

By July 2005, the Pony Express Snack Bar will be restructured and an updated menu will be offered its clientele. Absent since 1962, the remaining fir-carved cartoon panels will be "brought back to life" by restoration experts and returned to the snack bar.

Evidence of their gratitude, like a well-worn and beloved backcountry trail, will be erased by fresh maple boards in the Inn's centennial year.

Workers will carve out additional room for the first floor's renovated public restrooms from the snack bar's previous "ice cream space." Lobby wanderers will still be able to buy ice cream in the Pony Express, but it will probably be in the shape of "geyser bars."

The new registration desk will parallel the old check-in area, extending into the lobby. Its length will double, stretching northward into the 1927–1928 lobby extension area. To increase building stability, a log wall will replace one large plate glass window on the east wall behind the new desk. More convenient for guests, they will be able to check-in and make activity reservations at any of the new desk's seven "stations." All lobby projects will be complete by July 1, 2005.

The bell desk will remain in its current location. Like the new registration desk, a new hostess counter will be fashioned from volcanic rock and banded in wrought iron in keeping with other counters. The new desks' stone work will not bulge out at the base, making them more "user friendly." The location of the native stone water fountain or "bubbler" along the lobby's west wall will once again match views depicted in historic postcards.

During the last phase of the restoration, crews will tackle work necessary to maintain the exterior of the Old House. All types of weather —from sunshine to subzero temperatures and wind—have assaulted the Inn's exterior since the last major renovation in the 1980s. The Old House roof and related log work have deteriorated and will be replaced. Workers will add undetectable steel supports to the roof for protection against snow load and earthquakes. As a finishing touch, both wall and roof shingles will be coated with protective oil. (The rotted porte cochere floor will be replaced by July 2005.) No work will be done on the widow's walk except for the removal of the electrical wiring that powered the searchlights pre-1948.

Once again, the restoration will mirror the efforts of the Inn's builders a hundred years earlier—the work will be done in the off-season. Architects and contractors will brace the historic hotel and themselves against the challenges of winter. Beginning in mid-October 2004, the project is scheduled for completion by spring 2006 and will probably approach a cost of $20 million. Guests will continue to occupy Old Faithful Inn during the summer. The tell-tale process of appreciation will begin anew, and people will no doubt pause in the same spot that lobby guests did before them.[3]

The Old Faithful Inn in a heavy snow storm in February, with a spot of light showing the location of the sun behind the storm clouds, just above the peak of the building. *(Photos ©Jeff Henry)*

GEORGE AINSLIE—TODAY'S BLACKSMITH

distinctively with his own brand, unlike Colpitts's unsigned tools. One of Ainslie's first projects for the Inn was the dining room fireplace screen, the finishing touch for the fireplace rebuild of the late 1980s. He also hand-forged the hostess counter's ornamental iron band and rivets. Over time, some of Colpitts's work has unfortunately disappeared. Ainslie has fashioned replacement front porch lanterns and the decorative rivets that bejewel the Inn's counters and doors. He has also created about a hundred enormous spikes— foot long ¾" round nails with two inch heads—to keep the log stairs securely and safely fastened together.

Generations of people coming and going through the great entrance door had worn away over an inch of iron from its massive hinges by 1990. The exertion of two employ-ees was required to drag the door open in morning and shut in evening. Ainslie repaired the hinges by grinding them flat and inserting a bronze bushing to add the necessary bulk and keep the historical hinges operational. Before the early 1990s, Colpitts's massive key was "captured" in the door—never intended to be removed. It was operational, but chil-dren had swung on the key and eventually worn out parts of the lock works. Ainslie repaired the lock and used Colpitts's original key to forge a replica which now hangs on display inside the front door. The original key rests in the park's museum collection.

George Ainslie of Lavina, Montana earns a living as George Colpitts did in the early twentieth century, from forging iron. Crafting by hand, forge and anvil, Ainslie has created replacement wrought iron works for Old Faithful Inn as needed since 1989 and has established a kinship with Colpitts himself. Using original Colpitts creations, Ainslie has created molds that help him reproduce repli-cas that keep the Inn feeling whole. (He will likely forge iron for the Inn's 2004-2006 restoration project.)

Ainslie has crafted about half of the tools— tongs, shovel and pokers—around the great masonry fireplace. His tools are marked

Craftsmen of many trades keep the Inn's story alive through maintenance, repair, reproduc-tion and restoration, bless them all.

"The Inn will still move,
but will act as one,
instead of in pieces."

The Legacy of Old Faithful Inn

"You never really leave a place...part of it you take with you, leaving part of yourself behind."

—UNKNOWN AUTHOR

THE STORY OF OLD FAITHFUL INN'S FIRST ONE HUNDRED YEARS is riddled with talent, hard work and gratitude. It is the story of Yellowstone National Park, its preservation, the people who come to appreciate it, and the employees that make the experience memorable for the visitor.

Why did visitors of days gone by seek the wonders of Yellowstone? Why do people today still journey to the world's first national park? Unlike clothing or music fads, some things are always in vogue. Writer R. Paul Firnhaber has penned:

> *For even though our wilder origins have, for the most part, been acculturated out of us, there remains a strong unconscious memory of our connectedness with the earth. We return for mysterious and unspoken reasons, as if on a pilgrimage to a sacred place.*[1]

And Yellowstone National Park *is* sacred.

The Greater Yellowstone Area is a wild, relatively intact ecosystem resplendent with mountains forged by fire and ice, valleys cut by raging rivers of melted snow, uncommon geothermal unrest, and a myriad of plant and animal life. When the National Park Service was created,

If Yellowstone National Park is the crown jewel of the park system, then Old Faithful Inn is the crown jewel of its lodges.

Sunrise over the Yellowstone River. Photo ©Jeff Henry)

Bison at sunrise on geothermally warmed earth in front of the Inn. (Photo ©Jeff Henry)

preservation of these unique resources was one ingredient of the mandated balancing act. The equally important counterbalance was the enjoyment of the park's resources by people.

For generations, visitors have been magnetically drawn to Yellowstone National Park's extraordinary resources and have traveled from around the globe to experience Yellowstone by various conveyances: first by horse or foot; next by horse-drawn vehicle and locomotive; and later by bus, automobile, and recreational vehicle. To respond to increased Yellowstone visitation, entrepreneur Harry Child and his railroad backers, along with architect Robert Reamer and his team of builders gave Old Faithful Inn its genesis.

Reamer's Canyon Hotel sentiments hint of his earlier and likely aspirations for the Upper Geyser Basin hotel:

> I built it in keeping with the place where it stands. Nobody could improve upon that. To be at discord with the landscape, would be almost a crime. To try to improve upon it would be an impertinence.[2]

In Old Faithful Inn, Reamer blended modern comfort with charm, grace, and original rusticity. In his use of native materials and his ability to meet guests' expectations, Reamer's vision was simultaneously practical *and* grandiose. Analogous to the park's preservation and enjoyment directive, Reamer intuitively understood that success was realized through balance, years before the National Park Service was created. If Yellowstone National Park is the crown jewel of the park system, then Old Faithful Inn is the crown jewel of its lodges.

The influence of Old Faithful Inn has spread beyond the grateful folks who have actually admired and felt its native presence. Reamer's gift of architecture to the world was even more profound. The Inn stands as the first large-scale example of what is now called "parkitecture" or buildings that are designed to harmonize with nature. Because of that, Old Faithful Inn was a recipe of success that future national park architecture emulated. Park architects looked to their natural surroundings for inspiration and adapted their buildings to the tranquil scene the parks were there to protect. Many lodges crafted from native log and stone sprang up around the west as a tangible tribute to Reamer's triumph.

For many, a "cabin" stay is an inherently more memorable and rich experience than less imaginative accommodations made from cement and steel. The connection to nature for humans is an important one. It nourishes the soul, the spirit, the body, and the imagination.

Sunset over the Old Faithful Inn. (Photo ©Jeff Henry)

Since June 1904, pilgrims to the world's first national park have relaxed and reveled in Old Faithful Inn's simple luxuries after the day's exploration has revealed mysteries and evoked wonder. It is a great curiosity and comfort to dream of days gone by from a balcony settee or rocking chair scooted up to the secure glow of the Inn's fireplace. Old Faithful Inn helps the visitor in this task. Its stature, dignity, and pioneer "feel" transports the mind's eye back to an earlier, simpler time, linking today's guests with those of yesterday. This historic hostel makes the guest feel good and serves as a reminder that he or she is part of something bigger.

Old Faithful Inn is keeper of its secrets. Her wooden walls and floors sometimes creak and groan like lodgepole pines swaying in a Yellowstone breeze. Perhaps she will speak to you if you stop and listen with care. Few stories of the people who created and treasured the Inn a century ago have been told. Inn tour guide Betty Hardy said it well: "The Inn is a building of history and a building of mystery." Historians hope to uncover more of these mysteries of the Inn, but perhaps it is these untold stories that draw people to the bosom of the historical hotel.[3]

There are many descriptions of what the grand lobby of Old Faithful Inn looked like to visitors over the years and how it affected them. Writer Elizabeth Laden described the lobby this way:

> *Standing in the middle of the massive lobby is much like standing in the middle of a tall forest and trying to glimpse the sun through the tree branches....The place creaks as people walk over wood floors and up and down the staircases; it sounds like tree branches creaking in the wind.*[4]

"The Inn is a building of history and a building of mystery."

Jot down *your* impressions of the Inn and join a century of writers who have penned words to describe its effect on the human spirit and mind. Perhaps the Inn's greatest legacy for the future will be that many more people, affected by its presence and charm, will do the same.

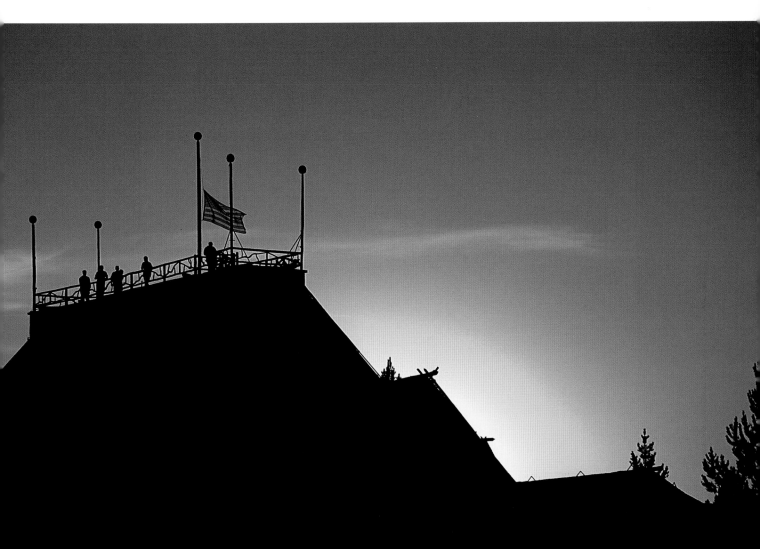

GLORIFIED LOG CABIN

Return, ye mighty builders,
Ye men of brawn, too few,
To witness: your dream in logs
Old Faithful Inn stands true.

Come see the mighty concourse
Of women, children too;
Knowing men, with eyes alight,
Who tribute pay to you.

Old Faithful Inn faithful stands,
A most befitting name,
A noble, sturdy structure
As lasting as its fame.

Return, ye mighty builders
In logs, come and review
Your glorified log cabin
Old Faithful Inn stands true.

By "Pete," the nightwatch. July 30, 1936.
To: R.C. Reamer, Architect and Builder,
And the men who worked with him
In 1903-1904.

—COURTESY JO ANN ZIMMERER HILLARD

INTRODUCTION

¹Friedrich Nietzsche, in Walter Kaufmann's English translation of "Der Fall Wagner," epilogue, 1888. The author thanks Dr. Duncan Large, Department of German University of Wales for locating the quote.

CHAPTER ONE – YELLOWSTONE'S HALLOWED EARTH

¹John Muir, *The Yellowstone National Park,* ed. William R. Jones (Silverthorne, Colorado: Vistabooks), 1999, pp. 61, 63.
²Shari Kepner, interview by author May 6, 2003. Kepner worked as Inn bellhop 2001-2003.
³See generally Robert B. Smith and Lee J. Siegel, *Windows into the Earth: the Geologic Story of Yellowstone and Grand Teton National Parks* (New York: Oxford Univ. Press), 2000; Robert B. Smith slide presentation, Mammoth, Wyoming, February 25, 2003; John M. Good and Kenneth L Pierce, *Interpreting the Landscapes of Grand Teton & Yellowstone National Parks: Recent and Ongoing Geology,* (Moose, WY: Grand Teton Natural History Association), 1996.

CHAPTER TWO – ENTICE, EXPLORE, PROTECT

¹Osborne Russell, *Journal of a Trapper,* ed. Aubrey L. Haines (Lincoln: University of Nebraska Press), 1965, p.99.
²Peter Nabokov and Lawrence Loendorf, *American Indians and Yellowstone National Park: A Documentary Overview,* (Yellowstone National Park: Yellowstone Center for Resources), 2002; Rosemary Sucec, Cultural Anthropologist, Yellowstone National Park [hereafter YNP], interview with author, September 24, 2002; Ann Johnson, Archeologist, YNP, interview by author, July 7, 2003.
³Aubrey L. Haines, *The Yellowstone Story,* Volume I (Boulder, Colorado: Associated University Press), 1977, p.35. Captains William Clark and Meriwether Lewis along with around 30 others made their historic journey west in 1804-06. While they did not discover Yellowstone, a portion of their party passed sixty miles north of the park. In August 1806, Colter was granted permission to be discharged from the expedition. He trapped beaver and traveled into what would become Yellowstone National Park in the winter of 1807-08 to promote a new trading post.
⁴Haines, *Yellowstone Story,* I, pp. 53-64.
⁵Richard A. Bartlett, *Nature's Yellowstone* (Albuquerque: University of New Mexico Press), 1974, pp.119, 188.
⁶Lee H. Whittlesey, *Yellowstone Place Names* (Helena, Montana Historical Society Press), 1988, p.115; Aubrey L. Haines, *Yellowstone Place Names, Mirrors of History* (Niwot: University Press of Colorado), 1996, p. 154.
⁷Carolyn Duckworth, ed., *Yellowstone Resources & Issues 2002* (Mammoth, Wyoming: Division of Interpretation, YNP, 2002, p.174.
⁸Bartlett, *Nature's Yellowstone,* pp. 194-210. The fruits of the Hayden Surveys include the breathtaking photographs of William Henry Jackson and the colorful interpretations of painter Thomas Moran. Visitors can relish their artistic interpretations of Yellowstone at the Albright Visitor Center at Mammoth Hot Springs.

CHAPTER THREE – WONDERLAND BECOMES A PLEASURING GROUND

¹Unknown author, "*Northern Pacific Railroad: the Wonderland Route to the Pacific Coast*" (Chicago: Northern Pacific Railroad [hereafter, NPRR]), 1885, pp. 24-25, Yellowstone National Park Research Library (hereafter, YNPRL), Mammoth, Wyoming.
²Whittlesey, *Place Names,* p.166.
³Aubrey L. Haines, *Yellowstone Story,* II (Boulder: Colorado, Associated University Press), 1977, p. 53-59.
⁴*Ibid.,* pp.102, 478. In 1889, Montana attained statehood seventeen years after the park was established. One year later, Wyoming and Idaho earned that status.
⁵J. A. Phillips III, "From A to Z with Warren McGee," *The Mainstreeter* (Bellevue, Washington: The Northern Pacific Railway Historical Association), Winter 1999, #18, pp. 6 & 7; Craig Reese, "The Gardiner Gateway to Yellowstone," *The Mainstreeter,* Spring 1996, # 15, pp. 5-21.
⁶Richard A. Bartlett, *Yellowstone: A Wilderness Besieged* (Tucson: University of Arizona Press), 1985, p. 63. Richard C. Overton, *Burlington Route: A History of the Burlington Lines* (New York: Alfred A. Knopf), 1965, p. 233. The author thanks Carol R. Mathews of the Park County Historical Archives in Cody, Wyoming.
⁷NPRR brochure, *Yellowstone National Park 1906,* p.12, Montana Historical Society Archives (hereafter, MHSA), Helena, Montana.
⁸Bartlett, *Wilderness,* p. 63-65; Haines, *Yellowstone Story,* II, p.123.
⁹Haines, *Yellowstone Story,* II, p.120. The Shack Hotel had 96 "rooms." "Capacity of Hotels," [1903], Northern Pacific Railroad collection, President's Subject Files, File 210A, Folder 11, Minnesota Historical Society (hereafter: MNHS), St. Paul, Minnesota. The author is grateful to Lee Whittlesey for access to all MNHS materials cited herein.
¹⁰Haines, *Yellowstone Story,* II, p. 116.
¹¹*Ibid.,* p. 119.
¹²A. Berle Clemenson, "Historic Structure Report, Old Faithful Inn, Yellowstone National Park, Wyoming" (Denver: Historic Preservation Branch, National Park Service (hereafter, NPS), p.5, YNPRL. Harry Child II, letter to author July 23, 2003. Child has in his possession the minutes of the Board of Directors of the Yellowstone Park Association. Mr. Bihler and his plans are from the December 6, 1897 entry.
¹³Haines, *Yellowstone Story,* II, p. 119; *Report of the Superintendent of the Yellowstone National Park to the Secretary of the Interior* (hereafter, *Report of Supt.*), 1899 (Washington, DC: Govt. Printing Office), 1899, p.5, YNPRL; Clemenson, "Report," p.5.

CHAPTER FOUR – THE NORTHERN PACIFIC RAILROAD AND HARRY CHILD

¹B.C. Forbes, *Men Who are Making the West* (New York: BC Forbes Publishing Co), 1923, p 324, Burlingame Special Collections, Montana State University (hereafter, BSC, MSU) – Bozeman Libraries.
²Bartlett, *Wilderness,* pp.174-176. Haines, *Yellowstone Story,* II, pp. 49, 50. Mark Daniel Barringer, *Selling Yellowstone, Capitalism and the Construction of Nature* (Lawrence: University Press of Kansas), 2002, pp. 57, 58. Delaware North Parks Services operates the park's store concessions (Yellowstone General Stores) as of 2003.
³Bartlett, *Wilderness,* p.175; Forbes, *Men,* p. 329.
⁴*Livingston Enterprise,* February 5, 1931, p.1. also February 6, 7 & 11, 1931, Livingston Park County Library (hereafter, LPCL), Livingston, Montana. February 11 article on Child's will mentions minor bequests left to family and several employees. *Report of the Supt.,* 1931, p.2, notes Child's death.

CHAPTER FIVE – THE CHILD AND REAMER TEAM

¹Forbes, *Men,* p.332.
²Lawrence Kreisman, "Robert Chambers Reamer," Unpublished paper, University of Washington, 1977, p.5, YNPRL; David A. Naylor, "Old Faithful Inn and its Legacy: The Vernacular Transformed," Cornell University Master's Thesis, May 1990, p.47, YNPRL; Bartlett, *Wilderness,* pp.180-181.
³Harvey H. Kaiser, *Landmarks & the Landscape: Historic Architecture in the National Parks of the West* (San Francisco: Chronicle Books), 1997, p. 132.
⁴David Leavengood, "A Sense of Shelter: Robert C. Reamer in Yellowstone National Park," *Pacific Historical Review,* 1985, p.511. Besides the Old Faithful Inn, other lasting Reamer buildings include: The Child residence in Mammoth, built 1908; Child's garage near the arch in Gardiner; Lake Hotel 1900-1903 modifications and East Wing 1922; National Hotel Wing 1936 (now main wing Mammoth Hotel); Mammoth Hotel Cottages 1938; Upper Hamilton Store, Old Faithful, 1929; Norris Soldier Station 1908; Green Meadow Ranch bunkhouse and blacksmith shop in Helena, Montana. Haines, *Yellowstone Story,* II, p.229. Haines claims the "Roosevelt Arch" in Gardiner was conceived by Hiram Chittenden and designed by Reamer. However, historians have not unearthed any supportive documentation. "Robert C. Reamer Drawings" in the F. J. Haynes Blueprint/Map Collection, MHSA. Brian Shovers, MHS, letter to author March 5, 2003, (re: Green Meadows Ranch).
⁵Jane (Reamer) White in Kreisman, "Reamer," p. 15; Bartlett, *Wilderness,* p.182.
⁶Clifton Daniel, ed., *Chronicle of the 20ᵗʰ Century* (Mount Kisco, NY: Chronicle Publ., Inc.), 1987, p.53-62.
⁷"New Hotels," *Gardiner Wonderland,* February 20, 1904, YNPRL.

CHAPTER SIX – THE CONSTRUCTION OF OLD FAITHFUL INN

[1]Robert C. Reamer, quoted in "W.H. Merriam Talks to Butte Evening News about Park," *Gardiner Wonderland*, March 23, 1905.

[2]Clemenson, "Report," pp. 6, 7.

[3]Robert C. Reamer, "Old Faithful Tavern, Yellowstone National Park," 1903, F.J. Haynes Blueprint/Map Collection, MHSA; *Livingston Enterprise*, February 13, 1904.

[4]Harry Child II, letter to author July 23, 2003. Child unearthed these loan figures and dates from YP Assoc. minutes in his possession. Clemenson, "Report," p. 10.

[5]"Upper Basin Station Journal," Army Records, Bound Vol. #188, p.110, YNPA. On June 12, 1903, acting Supt. Major John Pitcher left Fort Yellowstone "for trip to Upper Basin to regulate cutting of logs for Hotel by Y.P. Assoc." Journal of the Acting Superintendent 1903-1921," p.8, YNPA. Thomas Hallin, interview by author April 8, 2003. "Hotel and Machinery Record," October 2, 1892, p.50, Box YPC-151, YNPA.

[6]Clemenson, "Report," pp .6-8. Further hard evidence has not been found of the winter hauling scheme. R.C. Reamer to C.B. Power, February 16, 1911, MC55a, File9, Fldr1, MHS. Roy Renkin, interview by author May 13, 2003. Renkin has worked since 1979 in the park, since 1989 as Vegetation Management Specialist.

[7]"Upper Basin Journal," May 14-15, 1904, p. 178.

[8]R.C. Reamer to C.B. Power, February 1911, MC55a, File 9, Folder 1, MHS.

[9]*Livingston Enterprise*, January 28, 1904; J. H. Raftery, *A Miracle in Hotel Building – The Dramatic Story of the Building of the New Canyon Hotel in Yellowstone Park* (No place: no publisher), n.d., [1911] pp. 3-5, YNPRL.

[10]Susan C. Scofield and Jeremy C. Schmidt, *The Inn at Old Faithful, The Last Word in Hotel Building* (no place: Crowsnest Associates), 1979, p.11.

[11]Raftery, *Canyon Hotel,* pp.3-5; Edward H. Moorman, "Journal of Years of Work Spent in Yellowstone National Park 1899-1948," unpublished manuscript, April 2, 1954, p. 14, YNPRL.

[12]Raftery, *Canyon Hotel,* pp.3-5.

[13]Bob Berry, communication with author May 24, 2003. The authors thank Berry for a copy of his stereo card photograph.

[14]*Livingston Enterprise*, January 2, 1904. E.C. Culley traveled with blacksmith Colpitts.

[15]"Winter Tour of the Park," *Helena Daily Record,* January 28, 1904, MHSA.

[16]B. Riley McClelland, "Summary of Weather Data for Old Faithful, 1904-1960," YNPRL; Upper Basin Journal, October 1, 1903 to June 1, 1904.

[17]Ruth Quinn, "Old Faithful Inn Historical Tour," May 17, 2001. Quinn, employed by Xanterra Parks & Resorts, has led historical tours at the Inn since 1995. "Yellowstone Park Association (hereafter YPA), Annual Report, Season of 1903," NPRR, President's Subject file 209A, folder 3, MNHS. Ninety men were employed at Lake and the Upper Geyser Basin December 15, 1903, hence the "45" figure. Photo labeled "Old Faithful Inn Construction Crew," YELL 18746, Cab. 30, Box 18, Yellowstone National Park Photo Archives (hereafter YNPPA), U. S. Dept. of the Interior, National Park Service, Yellowstone National Park. In this photo, there are 50 men posed in front of the Inn.

[18]Scofield and Schmidt, *The Inn*, p.9.

[19]Nedward M. Frost, "National Register of Historic Places Inventory/Nomination Form, The Old Faithful Inn," NPS, Department of Interior (hereafter DOI), Washington, DC, June 27, 1973, [p.4], YNPRL.

[20]Thomas J. Hallin, interview by author December 10, 2002. Bernard O. "Pete" was Thomas's father. Bernard supervised all construction projects for Yellowstone Park Co., (hereafter, YP Co.), from 1919-1957. Thomas lived and worked in Yellowstone National Park from 1922-1960. Thomas worked for the YP Co. as assistant manager of construction from 1948-1958 and then as manager and V.P. of the company for two years. Myron Huntsman, interview by author January 22, 2003. Thomas J. Huntsman initially worked for Nelson Story, Bozeman cattle baron. He trained in Germany as wheelwright and wagon maker, but after 1882 turned to carpentry and built many Bozeman homes. During the Inn's construction, his son was serving an apprenticeship under him.

[21]F. Carmody, "note in flagpole" discovered summer 1954, YNPRL.

[22]Harry W. Child II, letter to author June 23, 2003. Betty Jane Oswald married Harry Child Sr.'s grandson, Huntley Child, Jr. The authors thank Harry W. Child II for passing on the story and for sharing his photographs and memorabilia.

[23]George Bornemann, interview by author January 27, 2003. Augsperger Scrapbook, YELL 18670, (Cab. 30, Box 18), YNPPA. Mark Watson, interview by author, November 5, 2000. Watson worked 20 years at the Inn in food and beverage, and maintenance; from 1997-2001 he worked as assistant maintenance manager. Darren Kisor, a member of the Historic Preservation Crew found the signature during a routine "glazing" inspection of the Inn's windows. The window was one of the Inn's original windows.

[24]*Gardiner Wonderland*, March 5, 1904. Golden Gate is a notch in the mountains through which the road to Old Faithful passes just five miles south of Mammoth Hot Springs.

[25]*Livingston Enterprise*, May 7, 1904. "Upper Geyser Basin, Old Faithful Inn," Haynes Papers, Coll. 1504, Box 156, Folder 31. Kreisman, "Reamer," p. 7. Reamer met Louise while she was visiting her uncle, Judge John W. Meldrum, U.S. Commissioner at Mammoth Hot Springs. The Reamers and daughter Jane moved to the Seattle area in 1921, to remain there until his death in 1938.

[26]Andy Beck, letter to author February 5, 2003. Beck was an architect for the Old Faithful Inn's Restoration Project in 1980-83. Beck works at Denver Service Center for the National Park Service. Dallas Profit, interview by Jeff Henry in 1980's. Profit was a YP Co. employee. Hallin, interview, April 8, 2003.

[27]"Old Faithful Inn," Jack E. Haynes papers and the Haynes Inc. Records, Collection 1504, Box 156, Folder 31, BSC, MSU. Quoted from *Haynes Guide* paste-up in above file.

[28]Andy Beck, ["The Inn, The Park and Other Things"] slide show, September 26, 2000, Old Faithful, YNP.

[29]David L. Leavengood, "Robert C. Reamer, Architect in YNP and Montana," unpublished manuscript, [1983?], p.4, YNPRL.

[30]Lee H. Whittlesey, interview by author June 16, 2003. L. Whittlesey has worked in the park since 1969; he became Yellowstone National Park Historian in 2002.

[31]Reamer, "Old Faithful Tavern," blueprint, MHS.

[32]Clemenson, "Report," p.47; L. S. Harrison, "National Register of Historic Places Inventory-Nomination Form" NPS, DOI, p.65, YNPRL.

CHAPTER SEVEN – THE INN'S FINISHING TOUCHES

[1]*Gardiner Wonderland*, March 5, 1904.

[2]Hallin, interviews December 10, 2002 and April 8, 2003. Tom remembered his father, Bernard "Pete," tell the "shingle instruction" story. Roy Renkin, interview by author May 6, 2003.

[3]Richard J. Dysart, "George W. Colpitts – A Livingston Blacksmith," in *In Celebration of our Past* (Bozeman, Montana: Gallatin Historical Society), November 2, 2002, pp.5-6.

[4]Ibid., p.11; *Livingston Enterprise*, May 14, 1904; Robert and Duane Shelhammer, interview by author, January 25, 2003.

[5]Scofield and Schmidt, *Inn*, pp.17, 20. "Yellowstone Park Hotel Company (hereafter YPHC), Vol. 3 *Inventory*" (Milwaukee, Wisconsin: The American Appraisal Co.), 1929, p.259, YNPPA. The author thanks Susan Kraft for assistance. *Livingston Enterprise*, May 14, 1904, September 4, 1909 and October 10, 1937.

[6]Clemenson, "Report," p.10.

[7]Ibid.; Bartlett, p.183. Christian G. Carron, in *Limbert Arts and Crafts Furniture, The Complete 1903 Catalog* (New York: Dover Publications, Inc.), 1992, pp. v, vi. The Arts and Crafts movement began in the mid–nineteenth-century in Great Britain. Simple "back to nature" Mission-style furniture was factory produced in the United States, but some handwork was still necessary.

[8]*Livingston Post*, May 17, 1904 and May 27, 1904, Yellowstone Gateway Museum, Livingston, Montana.

[9]Numerous F.J. Haynes postcards show early day furnishings. Haynes Collection, Montana Historical Society Photograph Archives, (hereafter MHSPA), MHS; "YPHC Inventory," 1929, pp.250-269.

[10]Ibid.; Ruth Quinn, interview by author January 23, 2003.

[11]"YPHC Inventory," 1929, pp.250-269; Clifford Paynter Allen, "Pilgrimage of Mary commandery no. 36, Knights Templar of Pennsylvania to the

Twenty-Ninth Triennial Conclave of the Grand Encampment U.S. at San Francisco, California," Part 5, August 28, 1904, p.43, Library of Congress, American Memory Collection, (http://memory.loc.gov).

[12]*Report of the Supt.1921*, p.44; James R. McDonald, "Old Faithful Inn, YNP, Historic Structure Report," May 1994, p.26.

[13]Clemenson, "Report," p. 121; Mary Murphy, interview by author February 7, 2003. Murphy is Business Analyst, Business Management Office, YNP, Mammoth, Wyoming.

[14]Grammar of Ornament Inc., "Sisal Area Rugs," [c1980], p.1, courtesy George Bornemann. Bornemann loaned the authors his personal files on the Old Faithful Inn and Robert C. Reamer, for which they are grateful. Bornemann worked at the Inn sixteen years as housekeeper, bartender, bellman, bell captain, assistant manager and finally, as manager in 1996-1997. *YPHC Inventory*, 1929, pp. 350-361.

[15]Bartlett, *Wilderness*, p. 183; *YPHC Inventory*, 1929, pp.287.

[16]Samuel Preston Ewing, "A Trip to Yellowstone Park 1904," unpublished manuscript, p. 2, YNPRL; R.C. Reamer to C.B. Power, May 11, 1911, MC55a, File 9, Fldr. 1, MHS; *Livingston Enterprise*, July 23, 1904; *Livingston Post*, May 17, 1904, p.1.

[17]Rodd L. Wheaton, "Architecture of Yellowstone – A Microcosm of American Design," *Yellowstone Science*, Vol. 8, Fall 2000, p.19. Robert C. Sahr, *Consumer Price Index Conversion Factors, 1800-estimated 2012*, www.orst.edu/Dept/pol_sci/fac/sahr/sahrhome, The author thanks Dr. Shannon V. Taylor, MSU Bozeman.

CHAPTER EIGHT– THE PRESENCE OF OLD FAITHFUL INN

[1]Cathy (Baker) Dorn, "YP Former Employees Newsletter – 2001," compiled by Homer Rudolf, www.richmond.edu/~hrudolf. Dorn worked in the Inn's Indian Gift Shop in 1970.

[2]Leavengood, *Sense of Shelter*, p.503.

[3]Roderick Nash, *Wilderness and the American Mind*, Revised Ed. (New Haven: Yale Univ. Press), 1978; Charles Francis Adams, *What Jim Bridger and I Saw in Yellowstone Park* (no place, no publisher), [1912-1914], p.13, Ayer Collection, Newberry Library, Chicago.

[4]Allen, "Pilgrimage," p. 42. The observation platform was measured by the Historic Preservation Crew in 1994.

[5]Scofield and Schmidt, *The Inn*, p. 19. Tom Morrisey, "Old Faithful," *Stamp World*, April 1983, p.81, YNPRL. There are some inconsistencies in this article, but the narrative seems to have credibility.

[6]Whittlesey, *Album*, p. 62. Clemenson, "Report," p. 36. Clemenson used c. 1910 photos from Henry Ford Museum. McDonald, "Report," p.29. "Haynes postcards," Haynes Collection, MHSPA. Several postcards from after 1927 clearly show six flags. F. Carmody, "note in flagpole". "Park Workers Fall into Hot Pool; One Dies," *Livingston Enterprise*, August 23, 2000. Hulphers, an Inn employee dining room worker, suffered third-degree burns and died after accidentally falling into Cavern Spring, Lower Geyser Basin.

[7]Haines, *Yellowstone Story*, II, p.120; Clemenson, "Report", p. 11.

[8]Robert Mautino, interview with author February 12, 2003. Mautino worked at the Old Faithful Inn 1956-60. A senior bellhop who had worked at the Inn since after WWII told him that in 1948 visitors could gain access to the above areas only with a bellman. Previously children had played, run on the upper stairs & landings and occasionally dropped things to the lobby below creating a safety hazard. Homer Rudolf, interview with author March 14, 2003. Rudolf worked a total of 14 summers from 1956-1974; his favorite job was bartender. Rudolf keeps employee (savage) stories alive through his web page, (see note 1, above).

[9]David Arthur Naylor, "Old Faithful Inn and its Legacy: the Vernacular Transformed," master's thesis, Cornell University, p. 50, YNPRL.

[10]Olin D. Wheeler, *Wonderland '96*, (St. Paul: Northern Pacific Railroad), 1896, p. 57, YNPRL.

[11]*Report of Acting Supt.*, 1904, p.10, YNPRL.

[12]Detroit Publishing Company, "The Porch, Old Faithful Inn, Yellowstone Park," 1909, postcard #12537, courtesy Jo Ann Hillard.

CHAPTER NINE – OLD FAITHFUL INN WELCOMES ITS GUESTS

[1]Allen, "Pilgrimage," p. 38.

[2]William E. Curtis, "More of the Park," *Livingston Enterprise*, September 4, 1909, p. 1.

[3]R. Quinn, Inn historical tour.

[4]Reamer, "Old Faithful Tavern" blueprint. Jeff Henry measured the lobby's interior height using a 100' tape, good knots, and for a weight: one of his Nikon cameras. Floor to peak measured 76', 10" on January 20, 2003. Henry tallied 26 steps to widow's walk platform on exterior stairway. Karen Wildung Reinhart counted 102 steps to uppermost landing before exterior door to widow's walk on April 19, 2003.

[5]Clemenson, "Report," p. 71. Gary Gebert, letter to author, February 24, 2003. Gary Gebert, "YP Newsletter: 2000," compiled by Homer Rudolf, note Ch. 8. Gebert worked as a bellman at the Inn from 1969-1980.

[6]Allen, "Pilgrimage," pp.38, 45.

[7]Mary Murphy, interview, February 7, 2003. James R. McDonald, "Old Faithful Inn 'Old House' Renovation Historic Structures Report" (Missoula, Montana: A & E Architects), 2001, p. 241 and "Executive Summary," p. 5. The author thanks Murphy for access to the above report and its blueprints. Jeff Henry measured the fireplace base on all four sides on May 7, 2003: 15'2" (N), 15'2" (E), 16'5" (S), and 15'5" (W). 15'6" is the average width.

[8]Clemenson, "Report," p. 71.

[9]McDonald, "Summary," p. 4.

[10]Olin D. Wheeler, *Wonderland 1905*, p. 57, YNPA. Adams, *Jim Bridger and I*, p.13. Jane MacMillan, "Hotels of Wonderland Restore Broken Appetites," *Helena Daily Independent*, July 26, 1914, pp.15, 18. The author thanks Lee H. Whittlesey for a copy of this article.

[11]Dave Berghold, Mike Kovacich, Dick Dysart and Ruth Quinn, "New Life for an Old Faithful Clock," *NAWCC* (National Association of Watch and Clock Collectors) Bulletin, Vol. 44, April 2002, p.131-137; Bornemann, interview.

[12]Interestingly, the Old House rooms without bath have just kept up with inflation; 2003 room rates are $79.50, including tax. Sahr, *Conversion Factors*.

[13]R. Quinn, Inn tour; Clemenson, "Report," pp. 140-141.

[14]Al Chambard, interview by author May 24, 2003. The phones in the halls were installed c. 1970 to replace the bell system. Chambard worked three years as Inn bellman and five as bell captain (1970-1977).

[15]Don Shaner, interview by author, February 26, 2003. Shaner was bellman and luggage porter at the Inn from 1954-1963.

[16]Yellowstone Park Hotel Co. "Rates on this Room," YPC-96, YNPA. A rate card indicated "3 rings" was a request for hot water, necessary before sinks with hot and cold running water were added to rooms in 1924.

[17]Pierre Martineau, interview by author February 21, 2003. Martineau worked as bellman, bell captain and finally "supt. of service" at the Inn from 1959-1970. Robert Mautino, [Yellowstone Park Employees Newsletter], compiled by Sally Anderson Thompson, June 6, 1987, p. [6], courtesy Chuck Lewis.

[18]Mary Murphy, interview by author March 25, 2003.

[19]*Gardiner Wonderland*, September 17, 1903; March 9, 1905; *Livingston Enterprise*, August 20, 1904.

[20]YPA, "Statement of Operating Results," 1904, MC 141, Box 4, Fldr. 8, MHSA.

CHAPTER TEN – THE CHARM OF OLD FAITHFUL INN – DINING, DANCING AND MORE

[1]Mrs. Edward H. Johnson, [Ruth C. Stockman], "Diary of Trip through Yellowstone Park – 1905," [1905], YNPRL.

[2]"Old Faithful Inn," Haynes Collection 1504, Box 156, Folder 31, BSC, MSU. The bell also announced important events. "Hotels," *Helena Daily*, July 26, 1914, pp.15, 18. Murphy, interview March 25, 2003. A refashioned c.1904 bellman's uniform will be displayed near the bell desk as part of the 2004-2006 restoration project.

[3]Annie Bucklee, letter to her mother, August 1, 1905, Collection 2385, BSC, MSU.

[4]Clemenson, "Report," pp. 140-141.

[5]*Ibid.*; James McDonald, interview by author April 18, 2003. Hardy, interview. Hardy revealed that the partition has been called "Fort Apache" for a long time.

[6]Clemenson, "Report," pp. 140-141; "no author," *The Willow Ware Pattern used at the Old Faithful Inn Yellowstone Park* (Chicago: Burley & Co.), n.d., Jack Davis Collection, YNP Museum.

[7]See generally YPHC and YPCo., "Accommodations and Services," 1930s-1970s, Rare Box 13, YNPA. "Menus," Haynes Papers, Coll. 1504, Box 65, Folder 10, BSC, MSU. Shaner, interview. Jo Ann Zimmerer Hillard, interview by author May 8, 2003. Hillard said by 1963 daily menus were not printed. Hillard worked as the Inn's Front Office Cashier (1963) and Auditor (1964-1965). The authors thank Hillard for access to her historic YNP postcard collection. Charles "Moon" Mullins, letter to author May 10, 2003. He worked in the dining room in 1966 and 1967; in 1968 he worked in the bar and was a bellhop in 1971 and 1972.
[8]"Menus," Haynes Papers.
[9]John A. Hill, "Report on Inspection of Yellowstone, Glacier, Rainier, Crater Lake and Yosemite Parks," DOI, 1916, YNP Central Classified file, 1907-1949, Record Group 79.3.1, National Archives & Records Administration, Washington, D.C.. "Statement," 1904, MC 141, Box 4, Fldr. 8, MHSA.
[10]Hill, "Report," p.10; Elbert and Alice Hubbard, A Little Journey to the Yellowstone Park, (New York: Elbert Hubbard), 1915, pp. 17-18, YNPRL. H.W. Child to Mr. Elliot, May 19, 1913, NPRR, President's Subject File, File 210C, MNHS. Mrs. Underwood managed the Inn in 1913 as well.
[11]John Landrigan, interview by author, May 7, 2002. Hillard, interview by author March 19, 2003. Names written near balcony are: H.C. Adkins; Edwin Davis, violin; Rollie Ische, pianist; E.L. Moche, drums (1924); Harry Adkins, G.E. McMurphy, drums, Henry Sugar, violin, Ernie [?] Moon, drums (1926); an additional name seems to have been added later.
[12]Florence E. Scott, Through the Yellowstone with Paul and Peggy (New York: Hurrt & Company), 1916, pp. 218, 219, YNPRL.
[13]Eleanor Hamilton Povah, interview by authors July 27, 2003. Eleanor (Ellie) spent twenty summers (1921-1940) living with her parents, Charles and May at Hamilton's Lower Store next door to Old Faithful Inn. Eleanor is the surviving matriarch of the family that operated Hamilton Stores, Inc. in Yellowstone from 1915-2002.
[14]Allen, "Pilgrimage," p. 46. Clemenson, "Report," p.71. Gebert, letter. Gary's father Fred played drums, and doubled as Lodge bell captain. In the early 1930s, the band played at Chicago speakeasies in winter.
[15]Allen R. Crawford, interview by author, February 3, 2002. Crawford was a Haynes, Inc. employee in 1937 and 1938 at the Old Faithful Inn. Yellowstone Park Company, "What to do at Old Faithful," c1936, and "Services: Old Faithful Inn," 1967, YNPRL. Lee Whittlesey, interview by author, March 24, 2003. Whittlesey noted the "occasional entertainment" was gone by 1969.
[16]Report of the Supt., 1940, p. 27; "Organ at Old Faithful Inn, William Fitzpatrick," Jack E. Haynes photograph, Box 158, #40342, MHSPA.
[17]Judith Turck, interview by author January 25, 2003, Billings, Montana. Gaylord Milbrandt, interview by author December 5, 2002. He served as a bellman at the Old Faithful Inn in 1958-59 and 2001-02. Robert Mautino, "YP News," [compiled by Sally Anderson Thompson], December 1988, [p.5], courtesy Chuck Lewis.
[18]Jeannie Shadoan Keeter, interview by author March 12, 2003. She played in 1965 and 1966; the last year, like Turck, she played her own organ. Charles "Moon" Mullins, "YP Newsletter 2002," note Ch. 8.
[19]George Sanborn, interview by author April 8, 2003. Another pianist served as relief musician for Sanborn.
[20]Jim Cole, interview by author, March 17, 2003. A music teacher for 23 years, Cole is still known to boom out a splendid melody or two from the second floor balcony.
[21]Donna Reed, interview by author May 11, 2003. Jim and Donna Reed are from Casper, Wyoming.
[22]Cole, interview. Rudolf, interview. Hillard, interview and letter to author March 28, 2003. The author thanks Hillard for photos of the groups' album covers. Jeff Henry, interview by author May 9, 2003.
[23]"Western Governors Visit Park; Reagan in Spotlight," p.1 and "Singing Waitresses and Waiters at Old Faithful Inn Add Vocal Spice by Perpetuating Tradition," p.5, The Yellowstone Cub, July 14, 1967, courtesy Jo Ann Hillard.
[24]Rudolf, interview; Michael V. Wurm, "A Historical Tour of Old Faithful Inn," script of NPS interpretive program, c.1974, YNPRL; Shari Kepner, interview by author July 7, 2003.
[25]Yellowstone Park Transportation Company, Yellowstone Park Booklet, 1912, Sara P. Connette Rare Book Coll., Box 15, YNPA. Hill, "Report," p. 10. Allen, "Pilgrimage," p. 42. Reamer, "Old Faithful Tavern" blueprint, MHS. Rooms were allocated to many of these services in Reamer's original blueprints of the Inn, but no official mention until booklet and inventory above.
[26][Statement showing items kept on sale at Mammoth Hot Springs Hotel Newsstand], NPRR, President Subject File 209A, folder 3 (or Folder 210A, folder 13), MNHS.
[27]"YNP Concessions," Haynes papers, Coll. 1504, (Box 164, Folder 11), BSC, MSU; Clemenson, "Report," pp. 130-133.
[28]Allen R. Crawford, "A Conversation with Allen R. Crawford, Haynes, Inc. Employee, Yellowstone National Park, 1937-1940, August 1997," YNPRL. The author thanks Allen and Jean Crawford for a copy. Crawford, interview.
[29]John Kennedy, letter to author, April 13, 2003. He and his company supplied the Indian Gift Shop from the late 1970s through the early 1990s.
[30]Ibid.; Pawn serves as a banking system. Items are traded for a loan of cash and if not redeemed, becomes the property of the pawn shop. Cathy Dorn, interview by author April 9, 2003. The "Maria" pots were made by the late Maria Martinez of New Mexico's San Ildephonso tribe; her pots are still collected today. Evelyn Zimmerer, interview by author March 19, 2003. Zimmerer, now 98 years old, worked from 1964-1986 at Old Faithful, nineteen of those years at the Inn (4 years as dining room hostess and 15 at gift shop).
[31]Eric Robinson, interview by author April 29, 2003. Robinson is the Director of Retail/Purchasing for Xanterra Parks and Resorts, Mammoth, Wyoming.

A BELLHOP'S DREAM REALIZED (SIDEBAR)

[1]Nancy Ost, interview by author, March 28, 2003. Reverend Bill Young, interview by author, March 24, 2003. Rev. Young became head of Christian Ministry in YNP in 1983 after serving as a student minister at Old Faithful Inn in 1975 and 1976.

CHAPTER ELEVEN – OLD FAITHFUL INN HISTORIC RENOVATIONS

[1]Stephen T. Mather to Horace M. Albright, June 23, 1927, Box C14, File: Construction of Buildings, YPHC, YNPA.
[2]Haines, Yellowstone Story, II, pp. 478, 479.
[3]Clemenson, "Report," p. 103.
[4]Hallin, interview December 10, 2002.
[5]Monthly Report of the Supt., June 1920, p. 13 and October 1922, p.16, YNPRL; Clemenson, "Report," pp.108, 111, 124.
[6]Clemenson, "Report," pp.119-120; Murphy, interview, February 7, 2003.
[7]Clemenson, "Report," pp. 114, 115.
[8]Naylor, "Inn," p. 50.
[9]Clemenson, "Report," p.103; Correspondence between NPS officials, Reamer and Child, June 1927, Box C-14, File: Construction of Buildings, YPHC, YNPA.
[10]"YPHC Inventory," 1929, p. 139. Correspondence between NPS, Reamer, Child, June 1927. A "mansard" roof has two slopes on all sides, with the lower portion steeper than the upper one.
[11]Clemenson, "Report," pp.103, 108. Correspondence between NPS, Reamer, Child, June 1927. The construction company Teufel and Carlson, hired 200 men. Hallin, interview. Bernard O. "Pete" supervised YP Company West Wing activities. Scofield and Schmidt, The Inn, p.14. Beck, letter to author May 7, 2003. The building measurement does not include cribbing, roof overhangs and outriggers.
[12]Clemenson, "Report," pp. 111, 115, 116. "The Beguiling Bear Pit Cocktail Lounge," (no place, no publ.),[post 1938], YNPRL. YP Co., "Bar Menu —The Bear Pit," 1947, Box C33, File #900, YNPA. The etched wildlife on columns and ceiling trim in today's Bear Pit (the east dining room addition of 1927) appears to have been carved by Oehrle as well.
[13]Andy Beck, "The Greatest Log Cabin Restoration: The Old Faithful Inn, YNP, WY," National Park Service Stories, (no place: Beck), 1993, p.8. The author thanks Beck for a copy.
[14]Bill McMillon, Old Lodges and Hotels of our National Parks (South Bend, IN: Icarus Press), 1983, p.98, BSC, MSU; Clemenson, "Report," pp. 120,123.
[15]Marty Tobias, Director of Xanterra Lodging, letter to author, May 28, 2002. Tobias listed 87 "Old House" rooms, of which 8 have private baths. When the Inn's "tubs" went to "showers" is unknown. Tom Stone, interview by author March 14, 2003. Stone worked at Inn maintenance/plumbing from 1977-1984.

[16]*Ibid.*; Sahr, *Conversion Tables.*

[17]Lawrence C. Merriam to Superintendent, YNP, June 23, 1947, Box C-33, Public Utility Operation File, YNPA. [Correspondence between park and NPS officials], March 1948, Box C-37, File: Buildings, YNPA. Originally, a third of West Wing rooms did not have private baths, but today all rooms have a bath. McDonald, "Report," 1994, pp. 29-31; Quinn, interview; Hillard, letter to author March 23, 2003.

GHOST ROOMS, GHOST STORIES (SIDEBAR)

[1][Leslie James Quinn], "How Many Rooms in the Inn?," *Commentary Newsletter*, (YNP, WY: Amfac Parks & Resorts), July 1996, Vol. 11, pp. 4-8. L. Quinn has been Interpretive Specialist in Yellowstone since 1994. R. Quinn, Inn tour. Tobias, interview.

[2]Bornemann, interview by author January 27, 2003; L. Quinn, interview by author January 23, 2003; "Someone asked about YP ghost stories...," five Web chat pages, October 20-29, 2000, YNPRL.

CHAPTER TWELVE – RECREATION AND RESOURCES AROUND THE INN

[1]Bartlett, *Wilderness,* p.87.

[2]*U.S., Statutes at Large,* vol. 28, p. 73.

[3]Haines, *Yellowstone Story,* II, pp. 17,18, 107, 285-286, 390n28; Bartlett, *Wilderness,* pp. 19, 34; Whittlesey, *Album,* p.41; H. Duane Hampton, *How the U.S. Cavalry Saved Our National Parks* (Bloomington: Indiana University Press), 1971, p. 182.

[4]Whittlesey, *Place Names,* p. 70.

[5]*Ibid.,* pp. 102-103.

[6]Bartlett, *Wilderness,* pp. 196-197; Whittlesey, *Album,* p. 67.

[7]"Old Faithful Swimming Pool," Haynes papers, Collection 1504, Box 138: Folder 51. Hallin, interview. Hallin assisted with the demolition.

[8]*Report of the Acting Supt.,* 1907. "letters between Superintendent and Officer," documents 6967, 7040, Box 14, item 27, Army Records, YNPA. *Fishing Regulations,* (YNP: Visitor Services Office), 2002. Current fishing regulations forbid keeping any native fish species.

[9]Adams, *Jim Bridger and I,* p. 13. The Shaw & Powell (permanent camp co.) stagecoach that was previously in the Inn's lobby is now in the Old Faithful Lodge. The Inn's guests would not have traveled in that coach.

[10]Fanny Harris, "A Dream Come True—1908 and 1909," SC 1225, p. 27, MHSA; Nellie Ranney in Charlotte Dehnert's "1905 Diary Entries Recall Rigors of Wagon Trip to Yellowstone Park," *Wyoming State Journal,* November 1, 1979, p. 14, YNPRL.

[11]Adams, *Jim Bridger and I,* pp.15, 16. The musician was Willard Weihe of Salt Lake City.

[12]"Yellowstone National Park Travel," Haynes papers, Collection 1504, Box 169: Folder 11. During August and September 1915, nearly one thousand automobiles toured the park; 33% of these were Fords. Bartlett, *Wilderness,* pp.82-87.

[13]Bartlett, *Wilderness,* pp. 82-87.

[14]Haines, *Yellowstone Story,* II, p. 259.

[15]Sahr, *Conversion Factors;* R. Quinn, Inn tour.

[16]Haines, *Yellowstone Story,* II, pp. 367, 479; Barringer, *Selling Yellowstone,* pp. 98-99; YPHC, "Financial Report to Secretary of Interior," 1918, MC 141, Box 9, Folder 6, MHS.

CHAPTER THIRTEEN – BEHIND THE SCENES

[1]Allen, "Pilgrimage," p.43.

[2]YPHC, "Financial Report to Secretary of Interior," 1913, MC 141, Box 9, Fldr. 6, MHSA; "Contract between YPHC and Oscar Roseboro," May 1, 1926, MC 141, Box 9, Fldr. 11, MHSA.

[3]Hallin, interviews by author December 10, 2002 and April 8, 2003.

[4]*Ibid.*

[5]Mike Parshall, interview by author April 14, 2003. Parshall manned the boilers at Old Faithful Inn from 1977-1981; from 1982-1985 he worked as a furniture restorer in the park. Mark Watson, interview by author, April 14, 2003.

[6]Roberta Hurtt, letter to author February 23, 2003. Hurtt worked the Inn front desk 1969-70. Her step grandfather, Lewis Reifsteck, worked in the boiler room for many years. Parshall, interview. Jeff Henry, interview by author May 2, 2003.

[7]Stone, interview; Parshall, interview.

[8]YPHC Inventory, 1929, pp.501-567, 568, 575, 604; R.B. Dole, "Report on Sanitary Conditions in the YNP," June 20, 1914, p.63-64, Army Records, Box 56, Folder 161, YNPA.

[9]Dole, "Report," pp.62, 65; YPHC Inventory, 1929, p 575; "Hotels," *Helena Independent,* July 26, 1914, p.18.

[10]Stone, interview. Today's maintenance crew is 21 strong and serves the entire Old Faithful area. Beth Casey, letter to author, March 20, 2003. Casey is Director of Human Resources, Xanterra Parks and Resorts in Yellowstone. Her favorite work years (1990-1993) were spent as Inn Executive Housekeeper!

[11]Stone, interview. Gary Gebert, interview by author April 16, 2003. Michael Ayler, interview by author March 20, 2003. Ayler was an Inn bellman from 1966-1969. Denny Sutherland, letter to author June 16, 2003. Sutherland was the Structural Fire Chief, YNP from 1987-2002.

[12]"Old Faithful Hotels," Haynes papers, n.d., Coll. 1504, Box 156, folder 30, BSC, MSU. Hallin, interview. Chris Larcinese, letter to author, February 23, 2003. Larcinese worked at the Inn laundry in 1982 and waited tables there in 1984.

[13]Gwen Peterson, *"Yellowstone Pioneers, the Story of the Hamilton Stores and Yellowstone National Park"* (Santa Barbara, California: Sequoia Communications), 1985, p. 21. Anna Borgh in "YP News," Dec. 1988, compiled by Sally Thompson, p.2. Borgh was an Inn chamber maid in 1927-1928. Ginny Irvine, *2001 YP Newsletter,* note Ch. 8. Irvine was an Inn waitress in 1969 and 1970. Chris Larcinese, letter.

[14]Dole, "Report," p. 62; Yellowstone Park Company, "Old Faithful Inn," YPC 158, Folder 1, YNPA; Casey, letter to author, March 20, 2003.

[15]Casey, letter, March 20, 2003.

[16]Bob Adams, interview by author April 4, 2003. Adams worked as Inn bartender from 1946-47 & 1959-83.

[17]Casey, letter March 20, 2003. Ruth Quinn, interview by author, April 7, 2003. Betty Hardy, interview by author, April 16, 2003. Hardy worked in 1992 as Inn dining room cashier, and in 1993 and 1994 as hostess. She began giving Inn historical tours in 1995. The average number of people on the tours ranged between 25 and 50. Currently, tours are offered at 9:30 and 11:00 a.m., and 2:00 and 3:30 p.m.

[18]Karen Boucher Selleck, letter to author May 20, 2003. Selleck was a park ranger interpreter from 1982-87 at Old Faithful. Ruth Quinn, letter to author June 19, 2003. Tamela Whittlesey, interview by author April 8, 2003. T. Whittlesey gave tours in the Inn from 1990-1992. Hardy, interview.

[19]Casey, letter March 20, 2003.

[20]Shaner, interview. Rudolf, interview. During their tenures, the night auditor, watchmen and others lived in Bat's Alley. Bell staff lived in the boys' ("horse stables") dorm. Rudolf had five roommates. Gebert, interview. "List of Buildings owned by Interior Department," YNPRL. Three houses and stables were built in Upper Basin by Engineers in 1907.

[21]"Inn," Haynes, Coll. 1504, Box 156: Folder 30, 31. Hill, "Report," p. 10. John Egger, interview by Lee Whittlesey, January 17, 1981 at Gardiner, Montana. Egger was a Fountain Hotel employee.

[22]Shaner, interview; Dorn, interview.

[23]George Bornemann, interview by author March 30, 2003. Kitchen fans vibrated his dorm floor.

[24]Casey, letter to author March 22, 2003. The Laurel dorm was known earlier as Windflower dorm.

[25]Haines, *Yellowstone Story,* II, pp. 368-369.

[26]NPRR, "Savage Special," (St. Paul: Northern Pacific Railroad), 1952, YNPRL. Hallin, interview. Mautino, interview. Mrs. E. H. Johnson, "Diary." She mentions a five piece Chicago orchestra [Nuernberger Orchestra] in Mammoth, 1905.

[27]"Savages Triumph at Old Faithful Inn," *Billings Gazette,* August 9, 1962. [Letter from striking waitresses to management,] YPC 118, File: Old Faithful Walkout, August 7, 1962, YNPA. John Baumm to Chief Ranger, July 11, 1947, C-33, Public Utility Operation File, YNPA. Elizabeth A. VanderPutten, letters to author, February 24 & March 11, 2003. VanderPutten was a waitress at Old Faithful Lodge in 1962.

²⁸Concessionaire monthly statistics, 1992-2002, courtesy Tammy Wert, Visitor Services Office, YNP, Wyoming; Casey, letter to author, March 20, 2003.
²⁹Clemenson, "Report," p. 124. Hallin, interview. Mary Fenner, "YP Newsletter: 2000," note Ch. 8. Fenner worked ten years for YP Co.: she was Inn Coffee Shop manager from 1963-1965. *Annual Report of the Supt.*, 1982, YNPRL.
³⁰Robert Greer, interview by author April 29, 2003. Curtis was Robert's father. The author thanks Betty Hardy for passing on the story.
³¹Jacqueline and Bruce Calhoun, interview by author at the Old Faithful Inn, June 17, 2002. In 2002, they celebrated 50 years of marriage at Old Faithful Inn.

CHAPTER FOURTEEN – SAVAGE MERRIMENT
¹Warren McGee in Reese, "Gardiner Gateway," *Mainstreeter*, p.9.
²Peterson, *Hamilton Stores*, p. 21.
³Martineau, interview. Tim Miller, communication to author May 15, 2003. Henry, his dad, was an Inn bellman from 1926-1936.
⁴Martineau, interview.
⁵Al Chambard, interview by author May 6, 2003. Gebert, interview.
⁶Chuck "the Logger" Lewis, letter to author April 14, 2003. Lewis was Inn bellman from 1968-1976. Roxanne Bierman, interview by author April 29, 2003. Bierman worked as Inn bellman in 1980 and 1981, near the beginning of her 10 year park career. Kepner, interview.
⁷Bierman, interview.
⁸Fenner, Newsletter 2000, note Ch. 8; Ayler interview.
⁹Leslie J. Quinn, "Savage Christmas "...the best of times," *Yellowstone Science*, Summer 2001, pp. 2-5. Quinn suggested that "Savage Days" in July was replaced by "Christmas" in July which eventually moved to an August celebration. Rudolf, interview. *Monthly Report of the Supt.*, August 1921, p.1, YNPRL. "Ninety-One Years of Weather Records at YNP, WY, 1887-1977," YNPRL. A "severe snowstorm" July 2, 1921 (3.8" in Mammoth, with even more at other points in the park) closed park roads. Perhaps this is the storm that originated "Christmas" in Yellowstone. Allen Crawford, interview by author July 5, 2003. "Christmas" was not celebrated in the late 1930s.
¹⁰Miriam Johnston, "YP Newsletter: 2000," note Ch. 8. Miriam Johnston, letter to author March 13, 2003. Johnston became the park's first woman bus driver in 1972. She drove bus from 1972-1975. Dorn, interview. Mautino, interview. The tree in the Firehole River was not decorated in the mid to late 1950s.
¹¹Fenner, "Newsletter 2000," note Ch. 8. Fenner, postcard March 12, 2003. Keeter, interview. Cole, interview. Cole led the Christmas carolers from 1984-2001 and again in 2003.
¹²Hardy, interview. One year, Hardy dressed as Mrs. Santa Claus. Kepner, interview. Carlos Smith, interview by author May 12, 2003. The light bulb decorating had been an established activity prior to his employment (1998).
¹³Rudolf, interview. The nearby Lodge was more well-known for its regular evening entertainment. "Old Faithful Guitar Duo is First in Spirited Talent Finals June 19," *Yellowstone Cub*, July 14, 1967, p. 6. The winners proceeded to the park-wide contest held at Old Faithful Lodge Rec. Hall.
¹⁴Hillard, interview. Bellman Tucker Brooks was the p.a. system comedian. Lee H. Whittlesey, interview by author June 16, 2003. The bus driver was Lon Marshall. Gebert, interview. R. Quinn, interview April 7, 2003.
¹⁵Margaret (Pitts) Levy, "YP Newsletter—2001." note Ch. 8. Levy worked at the Inn in 1971and 1972; she manually connected phones by way of an old-fashioned switchboard.
¹⁶Shaner, interview. Martineau, interview. Gebert, interview. Brian Raines, "YP Newsletter – 2000," note Ch. 8. Raines worked at the Inn as busboy in 1970 and bellman from 1971-1974.
¹⁷Anna Borgh, "YP News."
¹⁸Ayler, interview.
¹⁹Johnston, letter. Hurtt, letter. Rudolf, letter to author May 6, 2003. Dorn, interview. Jeane Blackburn, [YP] "Newsletter, 1986," compiled by Sally A. Thompson, courtesy Chuck Lewis. Jeane Blackburn, interview by author May 16, 2003. Blackburn worked at the Inn Gift Shop in 1969.
²⁰Gebert, interview. Joe Swift, interview. The last bellmen's banquet was held in 1991; in later years banquet participants purchased tickets.
²¹Lewis, letter to author April 7, 2003; Kepner, interview.
²²Raines, "YP Newsletter—2000," note Ch. 8. Rudolf, interview. 100 savages attended the Old Faithful Inn reunion in 2002.

CHAPTER FIFTEEN – WINTER AT WONDERLAND'S INN
¹Beulah Brown, *My Winter in Geyserland* (no place: Brown), 1924, p.6, YNPRL.
²Morrisey, "Old Faithful," pp.78-83.
³Horace M. Albright to Stephen Mather, June 1, 1927, Box C14, File: Construction of Buildings, YP Hotel Co., YNPA.
⁴Mary Murphy, interview March 25, 2003.
⁵Haines, *Yellowstone Story*, II, p.199.
⁶E. J. Sawyer, "Death of Ranger Charles Phillips," *Yellowstone Nature Notes*, Vol.4, April 30, 1927, YNPRL; Lee H. Whittlesey, *Death in Yellowstone—Accidents and Foolhardiness in the First National Park* (Boulder, Colorado: Roberts Rinehart), 1995, pp.63-64.
⁷Unknown author, "Gardening over a Geyser," *Scientific American*, July 9, 1898, p.24, YNPRL.
⁸YPH Co. Inventory, 1929, pp. 568. This inventory claims greenhouse was 14'6"x 60'. "Greenhouse over Hot Spring is a Novelty of Yellowstone Park," no publ., [1913], NPRR, President's Subject File, File 210 B, MNHS. H.W. Child to Mr. Elliot, May 19, 1913, NPRR, President's Subject File, File 210 C, Fldr. 1. Hallin, interview.
⁹Brown, *Geyserland*, p. 4-8. Thomas J. Hallin, interview by author July 30, 2003. Warren McGee told Hallin that two of the Musser sons were named Harold and Howard.
¹⁰Cliff Hartman, interview by authors April 30, 2002. Hartman worked winters for YP Co. 1955-1961.

CHAPTER SIXTEEN – OLD FAITHFUL INN ADMIRERS: FROM PRESIDENTS TO EMPLOYEES
¹President Gerald R. Ford, letter to author, December 9, 2002.
²"U. S. Presidents visited YNP," Haynes papers, Collection 1504, Box 156, Fldr. 20, BSC, MSU; Bartlett, *Wilderness*, p.181.
³Whittlesey, *Album*, pp. 131-137. Bartlett, *Wilderness*, p.97. Carol Shively, letter to author, March 20, 2003. A park ranger in YNP since 1987, Shively has been Interpreter Supervisor at Lake since 1989. Ranger Francis "Jim" Pound met with Pres. Coolidge at the Inn. Anna Borgh, "YP News."
⁴Whittlesey, *Album*, pp. 131-137. President Jimmy Carter, letter to author January 2003. President Ford, letter. Gebert, letter. Joe "Popeye" Mitchell, interview by author March 28, 2003. T. Whittlesey, interview. Since 1993, she has managed VIP reservations. Roger Anderson, communication to author, May 29, 2003.
⁵Mitchell, interview.
⁶Shaner, interview. Mautino, interview. Hurtt, letter. Dorn, interview. T. Whittlesey, interview. "Yellowstone" (Universal City, CA: Universal Pictures), 1936, YNPRL. This murder mystery offered good Yellowstone and Grand Teton National Park views and interior shots of the Inn and its customers. "The Yellowstone Cubs" (no place: Walt Disney Company), 1961. The author thanks Roger Anderson and Carol Shively for access to the video.
⁷Edward Hungerford, "Progress in Transportation," *Travel*, June 1915, pp. 37-39, YNPR. "Instructions on artificial geyser," Haynes, Collection 146, Box 38, Folder 6, MHSA. Howard H. Hays, *An Appreciation* (San Francisco: Union Pacific), 1914, p. 4, YNPRL. http://bancroft.berkeley.edu/Exhibits/Looking/waycacouldbe.html, info on 1915 Panama Pacific International Exposition. "Programme of Music at Old Faithful Inn by the Official Exposition Orchestra" (no place: Union Pacific System), [1915], University of Wyoming Libraries in Laramie, Wyoming. The author thanks Tamsen L. Hert for forwarding a copy of the program.
⁸Walt Disney World, *Disney's Wilderness Lodge* (Lake Buena Vista, FL: Walt Disney World), 2001.
⁹Kathy Gallagher Summerfield, phone interview by author April 25, 2003.
¹⁰Glenn and Wanda Roberts, interview by author April 16, 2003 in Lewistown, Montana. They usually request room number 119.
¹¹Concessionaire stats, Visitor Services Office.

[12]Diane Chalfant, interview by author January 13, 2003. Chalfant has been Chief of Interpretation, YNP since 1998.
[13]Greer, interview.
[14]Beth Casey, letter to author March 22, 2003. Jo Ann Zimmerer Hillard, in Addison Bragg's "She Loves Park Inn's Every Log," *Billings Gazette*, June 20, 1965, courtesy Hillard. Joe Swift, interview by author May 2, 2003. Joe worked 1991-92 as bellman and 1994-98 on the Inn's Historic Preservation Crew. Lorraine was Inn Sr. Clerk in 1992 and bellman in 1994-95.

CHAPTER SEVENTEEN – BRUINS AROUND THE BASIN – BEAR STORIES FROM OLD FAITHFUL INN
[1]A. M. Cleland quoted in "New Rustic Hotel," *St. Paul Dispatch*, [1904], clipping in Hester F. Henshall Journal, MHSA. Cleland was general passenger agent for the Northern Pacific Railroad.
[2]"Upper Basin Station Journal," September 19-20, 1903, p.141-142.
[3]H.H. Tammen, Co., "Bears near Old Faithful," postcard #5375, courtesy Jo Ann Hillard; Allen, "Pilgrimage," p.42.
[4]Helen Clifford Gunter, "Yellowstone Park Three Times Around," unpublished manuscript, 1987, pp.10-14, YNPRL.
[5]Charles Phillips, "Doings of Bears," *Yellowstone Nature Notes*, Vol. 2, December 7, 1925, p.4, YNPRL.
[6]Dorr G. Yeager, "More about Baby Bears," *Yellowstone Nature Notes*, Vol. 8, April, 1931, p.28, YNPRL. Today, the NPS does not conduct or condone such intrusive research practices.
[7]Frank W. Childs, "Bears and Barbers," *Yellowstone Nature Notes*, Vol. 9, Jan-Feb 1932, p.8, YNPRL.
[8]Crawford, interview; Hallin, interview; "Hospitable Old Faithful Inn Turns Away Grizzly Guest," *Salt Lake Tribune*, August 22, 1937, courtesy George Bornemann.
[9]Bonnie McDougall Hammar, letter to Lee Whittlesey [July 27, 2003], p. 3, vertical files, YNPRL.
[10]Kerry A. Gunther, "Bear Management in Yellowstone National Park, 1960-1993," in *International Conference Bear Research and Management*, 1994, p.553, Bear Management Office, YNP, WY.
[11]Whittlesey, *Death*, pp.44-45.

CHAPTER EIGHTEEN – NATURE CHALLENGES OLD FAITHFUL INN
[1]Milbrandt, interview.
[2]Katherine Miller Jensen, interview by author April 19, 2003. Jensen waited tables at Lower Hamilton Store at Old Faithful in 1959.
[3]See generally Edmund Christopherson, *The Night the Mountain Fell: the Story of the Montana-Yellowstone Earthquake* (Missoula, Montana: Earthquake Press), 1966; Smith and Siegel, *Windows into the Earth,* pp.3-9, 17-21; Shaner, interview.
[4]Milbrandt, interview; Martineau, interview.
[5]Christopherson, *Earthquake*, pp. 14-15; Martineau interview; Chester O. Cantrell, "Old Faithful Area Report, Earthquake 1959," YNPRL.
[6]"Old Faithful Inn Closed for Now," *Montana Standard*, August 22, 1959, YNPRL; "Park's Heaviest Quake Damage at Old Faithful – Inn is Evacuated, East Wing and Main Lobby are Closed," *Billings Gazette*, August 19,1959, YNPRL.
[7]Mautino, interview; *Monthly Report of Superintendent*, August, September, November, 1959 [p.1 of each], YNPRL.
[8]Thomas J. Hallin to Lemuel A. Garrison, October 6, 1959, YNPRL; Clemenson, "Report," p. 121; Denise Stewart, "Old Faithful Inn Dateline," unpublished document, [post 1993],[p.4], courtesy Bornemann.
[9]Thomas Hallin, "Report on Earthquake Damages to YPC Facilities," October 1, 1959, Box D-196, File 3415, YNPA; Hallin, interview; Beck, "Restoration," p. 8.
[10]Christopherson. *Earthquake*, p.14; Milbrandt, interview; Jensen, interview.
[11]Scofield and Schmidt, *Inn*, p. 19. This myth has been perpetuated in many books and references; see also the sign on the gate that blocks access beyond the Inn's third floor. Mautino, interview, note Chapter 8.
[12]McClelland, "Weather Data Old Faithful;" Clemenson, "Report," p. 121. Hallin, interview. Beck, slide show, 2000. More settling probably occurred post quake. McDonald, interview, April 18, 2003.
[13]McDonald, "Report," 2001, Appendix A, p. 7; Wurm, "Historical Tour Inn."

CHAPTER NINETEEN – A FIRESTORM THREATENS OLD FAITHFUL INN
[1]Lee H. Whittlesey, "A Ranger Remembers the Fires at Old Faithful in 1988," unpublished manuscript, (1989 or 1990), Manuscript Collection, YNPRL.

CHAPTER TWENTY – THE INN RESTORED
[1]Beck, "Restoration," p. 1, note Ch. 11.
[2]"Grand Old Inn in Yellowstone Park." *Bozeman Daily Chronicle*, August 28, 1987.
[3]Haines, *Yellowstone Story*, II, p.120.
[4]Beck, "Restoration," p. 4; Beck, slide show, 2000.
[5]Beck, "Restoration," p 5.
[6]*Ibid.*, pp.2-4. A square = 100 feet.
[7]*Ibid.*, p. 9; Beck, slide show, 2000.
[8]Beck, "Restoration," p. 3.
[9]*Ibid.*, p. 8.
[10]*Ibid.*, p. 8. "Yellowstone National Park, Old Faithful Inn" (Denver, CO: Great Panes Glassworks, Inc.), 1988, YNPRL. Bornemann, interview, January 27, 2003. Jack Hardon carved his initials in the artwork.
[11]Beck, "Restoration," pp.4, 7-8; "Denver Firm Aids Faithful Restoration of Old Inn," *The Denver Post*, June 2, 1988.
[12]Andy Beck, letter to author December 4, 2002.
[13]Andy Beck, "White House Press Release of the Presidential Design Awards," memo to Paul Schullery, July 28, 1994, YNPRL. The National Endowment for the Arts award, the "Federal Design Achievement Award" was awarded the Inn in May 1992. Six months later, The "National Historic Preservation Award," awarded only once a quarter century, was presented to Old Faithful Inn in Washington, D.C.

CHAPTER TWENTY-ONE – THE 2004-2006 RENOVATION PROJECT – A BIRTHDAY PRESENT FOR THE INN
[1]John Ruskin, in *The Oxford Dictionary of Quotations*, Third Ed. (Oxford, England: Oxford University Press), 1979, p.411, vs. 22. Excerpt is from Ruskin's "The Lamp of Memory," Chapter 6, p.10.
[2]James R. McDonald, interview by author April 14, 2003.
[3]Murphy, interview by author March 25 and 26, 2003; Murphy, letter to author May 30 and July 16, 2003; See generally McDonald, "Report," 2001; James R. McDonald, interview by author April 14, and April 18, 2003.

GEORGE AINSLIE – TODAY'S BLACKSMITH (SIDEBAR)
[1]George Ainslie, interview by author February 12, 2003. Ainslie has owned and operated Prairie Elk Forge in Lavina, Montana for twenty years. McDonald, interview April 18, 2003.

CHAPTER TWENTY-TWO – THE LEGACY OF OLD FAITHFUL INN
[1]R. Paul Firnhaber and James Frank, *Rocky Mountain National Park Perspectives*, (Estes Park, CO: First Light Publishing), 1991, pp. 2-3.
[2]Robert C. Reamer in Raftery, *Canyon Hotel*, p. 7.
[3]Betty Hardy in "Old Faithful Inn Living Museum Talk," video produced by John and DeNette Landrigan, 1997, courtesy Betty Hardy.
[4]Elizabeth Laden, "Grand Old Inn in Yellowstone Park," *Bozeman Chronicle*, August 28, 1987.

© Jeff Henry   © Karen Reinhart

The authors have over forty years' cumulative experience in Yellowstone National Park. A native Montanan, Karen W. Reinhart has worked twelve years as a National Park Service Interpretive Ranger at Lake in Yellowstone. Jeff Henry has worked various jobs in Yellowstone: from fishing guide and ranger to winterkeeper and freelance photographer. Their knowledge and love of the park guarantee the reader an intimate look at one of the park's most beloved icons, Old Faithful Inn.